windows 98
made
painless

THIS IS A CARLTON BOOK

Text and design copyright © Carlton Books Limited 1999

A CIP Catalogue for this book is available from the British Library

ISBN 1 85868 835 3

Executive Editor: Tim Dedopulos
Production: Alexia Turner

Notice of Liability
Every effort has been made to ensure that this book contains accurate and current information. However, the Publisher and the author shall not be liable for any loss or damage suffered by readers as a result of any information contained herein.

Trademarks
Microsoft® and Windows® are registered trademarks of Microsoft Corporation. All other trademarks are acknowledged as belonging to their respective companies.

Printed and bound in Italy

windows 98

made
painless

Terry Burrows

CARLTON

CONTENTS

BITS AND PIECES

This may not apply to you, but to get things started we'll assume that not only are you new to Windows 98, but also that the idea of using a PC is still pretty novel to you. This chapter will provide you with a brief guide to the hardware components that make up your PC, such as the screen, keyboard and mouse. We'll also take a peek under the lid to look at the things that make a PC tick.

THE BASICS OF YOUR PC

Although you're certain to be itching to switch on your computer and discover the undoubted delights of Windows 98, let's just spend a few minutes going over some the basic components of your PC. This will also get you acquainted with some of those strange buzzwords that the "techies" like to baffle us with.

<u>VERY</u> BASIC STUFF

If you're reading a book about Windows 98 then you will either already own (or be thinking about owning) a PC. Those two letters stand for "personal computer". Although this could be seen as a generic term to describe all home computers, a PC (or "IBM compatible PC") is a special type of computer that works in a different way to others, such as the Apple Macintosh. PCs come in many forms, but irrespective of whether the logo on the casing says "Dell", "Tiny", "Time", or any of the hundreds of other well-known manufacturers, they are all PCs. All of the hardware and software designed for PCs should be able to work with EVERY model; software written for an Apple Macintosh will not work on a PC, and vice versa.

HARDWARE AND SOFTWARE?

Hang on a minute, what's all this "hardware" and "software" business about? OK, these are your first buzzwords. Every computer consists of hardware and software. The hardware is everything "physical" about your computer – the parts that you can see and feel. The software refers to the programs (sometimes called "applications") that make your computer function. Without software a computer is a useless piece of technology – it can't do a single thing!

Now let's take a quick look at the various pieces of hardware that make up your PC.

MONITORS

In the old days these were called VDUs (Visual Display Units). The monitor is the part of the computer that looks like a TV screen. Most monitors are powered independently of the main computer and so have their own on and off switches. Like TVs, most also usually have a set of controls for adjusting the contrast, brightness and sometimes the resolution.

The text and images you see on the screen are made up of tiny dots called "pixels". The greater the number of pixels that make up the picture, the more detailed the image. The screen resolution is measured in pixels. For example, "1024x768" describes a screen which is made up from 1024 pixels along the horizontal axis and 768 pixels along the vertical axis.

SYSTEM UNIT

The main "body" of the computer is called the system unit. This houses the PC's processing circuitry, hard disk, power supply and other hardware elements, such as floppy disk and CD-Rom drives. We'll talk about these parts a few pages down the line.

KEYBOARD

The keyboard is a standard typewriter-style keyboard that allows you to interact with the computer.

MOUSE

The mouse is used to move a pointer or cursor around the screen. For the most efficient use of your PC you should be able to use the mouse and keyboard in tandem.

Display icon   Keyboard icon   Mouse icon

PERIPHERAL DEVICES

The parts just described are what you can typically expect to find when you open the box that you've just brought home from your local PC store. There are, however, a number of other pieces of hardware that (if you're lucky) might well have been bundled-in with your purchase, or that you might have bought separately.

MODEM

A "modulator/demodulator" (modem for short) allows your computer to connect to the Internet via a domestic telephone line. This means that as long as you subscribe to an Internet service provider you can send e-mails and browse the World Wide Web. A modem can either be an external box that connects between your computer and the telephone or a piece of electronic circuitry that slots inside the computer's casing.

PRINTER

As you might imagine, a printer allows you to produce a paper version of the information on your screen. There are nowadays two basic types of printer – inkjet and laser. Both can produce excellent results, but for high-quality black and white output, laser is best. If you want colour printing, inkjet is the only practical possibility, since the laser equivalent is still prohibitively expensive for home users.

GAME CONTROLER

Games designed to be played on a PC can be controlled by keyboard or mouse (or a combination of the two). In many cases, though, they will work better with a specially designed joystick. They also prevent you wearing out the mouse buttons during rapid-fire games!

Modem icon

Printer icon

Game Controller icon

SCANNER

This operates rather like a photocopier in that you place a picture on a flat glass "bed" and scan the image into your PC. You can then change the image using a photo-manipulation program. You can get very cheap scanners these days which provide good enough quality images to use on a Web site.

EXTERNAL MEDIA DRIVE

Your PC will almost certainly come equipped with floppy disk and CD-ROM drives. These are two common storage "media". The drawback of "floppies" is that they can't hold very much data. If you want to transfer large files between different PCs you will need an alternative storage medium. Iomega's "Zip" cartridges can hold up to 20 times as much as a floppy disk; "Jaz" cartridges (by the same manufacturer) can hold almost 80 times as much as a floppy. These drives are usually connected externally by cable to your PC, although some PCs have them fitted internally with their floppy and CD-ROM drives. An alternative to a CD-ROM drive is a DVD drive. DVDs are the same size as a compact disc, but they can hold much more data.

CD-WRITER

With a CD writer you can transfer files to a recordable CD. There are two types of recordable CD: one that can only be used once (CD-R), and the more costly alternative that can be used many times (CD-RW). You need a special drive to be able to write information to a CD.

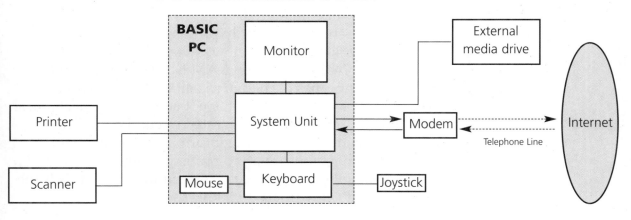

LET'S TAKE A LOOK INSIDE

You've seen the advertisements – you know, the ones that go something like "SuperPC presents the new 500MHz Pentium III complete with 32 megs of RAM and a 3 gig hard drive and...". What on earth does it all mean? Over the next few pages we'll lift the lid on your PC's system unit and describe some of these mysterious new terms.

STORING INFORMATION

There are two distinct forms of data storage used in all PCs. The first is the "hard disk"; the other one is called "RAM" or, to give it its full name, Random Access Memory.

You can think of the hard disk as being rather like your PC's own filing cabinet (indeed, when you use Windows 98, you'll see that you can take that analogy even further). It is a magnetic storage medium made up from a series of spinning disks. A small drive head moves across the surface of the disks to locate the data. When you switch off your PC, the hard disk retains the information stored – when you switch back on, your data should be unaltered.

RAM is different in that it only processes the information that you are working on right now. When you switch off your PC, everything that was held in RAM is lost. The reason for the two different types of memory is all to do with speed. Unlike hard disk memory, RAM is not accessed by mechanical means, but is a "chip" in an integrated circuit board. This means that it can read and write information many, many times faster. When you run a program, although it is stored on the hard disk, its functions are performed in RAM – this is the only way that it can work so quickly.

SAVE IT!

An understanding of these two different forms of memory underpins the first rule of computing – DON'T FORGET TO SAVE YOUR WORK! Imagine that you are writing a letter on your PC. You have launched a word processing program which is running in your PC's RAM. Everything you type remains in RAM until you perform the SAVE command. This makes a copy of your work in a file on the hard disk. If you switch off your PC before you SAVE, your work will be lost. If you QUIT from the program before you SAVE, your work will be lost (although at this point most programs will give you a prompt to ensure that you haven't forgotten). If you have a power failure or your computer "crashes" (they have a nasty habit of doing this at inconvenient moments), your work will be lost. You simply MUST get into the habit of saving your work at periodic intervals. If you are working on a lengthy document, don't let ten minutes pass without saving your file to the hard disk. That may sound like paranoia, but you won't think so when your PC crashes at the end of long day and ALL of your work has been irretrievably lost.

HOW SAFE IS THE HARD DISK, THEN?

Like anything mechanical, every type of memory device will stop working at some point. It's unlikely for a hard disk to fail within the first year of its life, but it's also not impossible. Therefore, the second rule of computing is ALWAYS MAKE A COPY OF YOUR WORK AWAY FROM THE HARD DISK. This process is called "backing up". By all means maintain your filing system on your hard disk, but always back up to another medium – cartridge, CD or an external hard disk drive. Which type you use will depend on your hardware and on the number and size of the files you create. Floppy disks may be large enough for simple text documents but audio or video files will need a medium capable of storing more data.

SIZE MATTERS

So how do you know if a storage device has enough space to hold a file that you want to copy? Every type of storage medium can be described in terms of how many "bytes" of data it can hold. A byte is the memory needed to store a single character or number. For example, if you use Windows 98's Notepad program to store the phrase "I am 35 years old", it will use up 17 bytes of the computer's memory (the spaces between the words also each take up a byte). A typical hard disk on a modern PC is capable of storing BILLIONS of bytes. The table below lists the terms that define data storage.

Definition	Abbreviation	Number of Bytes	
Kilobyte	K, KB	1,000	
Megabyte	M. MB, meg	1,000,000	(million)
Gigabyte	G, GB, gig	1,000,000,000	(billion)
Terabyte	T, TB, tera	1,000,000,000,000	(trillion)

If we look back at our "SuperPC" advert on the previous page, we can tell that it has a hard disk that can hold 3 gigabytes and that it can also hold 32 megabytes in its RAM.

Storage capacity varies for the other types of media. A list of maximum volumes is shown below. You'll see that a wide variation exists. Although very cheap, floppy disks are now becoming increasingly redundant to the point that some PC manufacturers don't install them as a standard feature. Their place has largely been taken by the Zip format. Although of similar physical proportions, Zips can hold vastly more data. DAT tape can be used to store very large volumes but is very slow: it also has to be read sequentially to load a specific file.

Media	Volume	
Floppy Disk	1.4 meg	1,400,000 bytes
Zip 100	100 meg	100,000,000 bytes
Zip 250	250 meg	250,000,000 bytes
Jaz	1 gig	1,000,000,000 bytes
CD	650 meg	650,000,000 bytes
Flipdisk	6.4 gig	6,400,000,000 bytes
DAT	30 gig	30,000,000,000 bytes
DVD-RAM	5.2 gig	5,200,000,000 bytes

ENDLESS CIRCLES

The rapid pace of change can be a nightmare for PC owners – within days of buying a brand new machine, something new and even better is certain to be unveiled. Avoid getting caught up in the desire to constantly upgrade your system. Ask yourself what you REALLY want from your PC. If you are a multimedia Web designer or video editor, the fastest tools will make your life easier; if you just want to type letters and occasionally browse the Web, a high-specification may be a waste of money.

PROCESSING POWER

Before we put the lid back on our PC, let's a take a look at the final crucial factor affecting a PC's perfomance – the speed of the microprocessor. Sometimes called the Central Processing Unit (CPU) or the "chip", it is the microprocessor that does all the hard graft. If you think of a computer program as a set of instructions that have to be worked through in a strict sequence (which is exactly what it is), the fastest processors will be able to perform the instructions the quickest.

Processing speed is measured in megahertz (MHz). At the moment the most powerful processors are the Intel Pentium IIIs, which are capable of operating at over 500 MHz. This is one of the many areas of the computer world that literally changes by the week. Only a few years ago, an Intel 486 processor running at 100 MHz would have been considered a luxury. Other recent processors make use of what is known as MMX technology, which improves performance when running multimedia programs or games.

BIGGER IS BETTER

When you are comparing storage volumes and processor speeds on different PCs, the rule is a simple one – the more you have of everything, the better it is! Unsurprisingly, though, bigger also means costlier. Before you decide to buy you should ask yourself if you really need all that power. If all you want to do is text processing, then the cheapest, most basic models on the market will be more than adequate. On the other hand, if you want to record audio or edit videos then anything less than 64 meg of RAM, a 5 gig hard disk and a 300MHz processor will make life tough.

WHAT ABOUT SOFTWARE?

You now know all about the hardware side of your PC, but what of the "software" we mentioned earlier? The only reason for owning a PC is so that you can run programs (another term for software). When you type a letter on your PC, you run a program; when you do calculations on your PC, you run a program; and when you play *House of the Zombies IV*, you run a program. Indeed, Windows 98 is also a program. So you can see that they're pretty important really! Here is a list of just some of the types of programs that can be run on a PC.

- **Word Processing**
- **Desktop Publishing**
- **Games**
- **Spreadsheets and accounts**
- **E-mail**
- **Browsing the World Wide Web**
- **Education and reference**
- **Drawing**
- **Recording and editing sound**
- **Animation**
- **Listening to music**
- **Graphic design**
- **Diary systems**
- **Manipulating images**
- **Digital photography**
- **Recording and editing video**

GETTING STARTED

1

This is where things start to move. We'll begin with a gentle introduction to Windows 98 and some of the things it's capable of helping you do. You will encounter the all-important Windows 98 Desktop – the area in which you'll do most of your day-to-day work. You'll also learn about the basic mouse and keyboard manoeuvres that will not only help you to get the most out of Windows 98, but most other programs as well.

WHAT IS WINDOWS 98?

Windows 98 is a program, but one that doesn't really do anything particularly interesting in its own right. Sounds great, doesn't it? In fact, Windows 98 is what is known as an "operating system". Without this type of software your PC can't run any other programs. Windows 98 is not the only operating system to exist, but is the most recent version of Microsoft's Windows, which appears on at least 90 per cent of the world's PCs.

WHAT DOES IT DO?

Apart from continuing to maintain Microsoft's domination of the world's software market, Windows 98 exists for just one reason – to make working on your PC as easy as possible. Using Windows 98 you can:

- Run other programs.
- Change the way your PC screen looks.
- Customise the way your PC works according to your own personal preferences.
- Organise, move, copy and delete data on your PC.
- Rapidly find lost or missing documents on your PC.
- Perform periodic maintenance on your hard disk to keep your PC working at optimal efficiency.

Whatever tasks we have to do, we all have our own preferred ways of going about them. Windows 98 has enough options to cater for the most diverse requirements. You'll find out how you can customise your PC in chapter 5 (pages 73-91).

HOW DO I MAKE WINDOWS 98 WORK?

Since your PC is a pretty useless piece of technology without an operating system, if you have bought a new PC you will find that Windows 98 has been pre-loaded in almost all cases. If you are upgrading from Windows 95 or an older version of Windows, you will need to install Windows 98 from scratch from your CD-ROM. Turn to pages 160-163 for more details on installation. Otherwise, all you have to do is turn on your PC and watch Windows 98 burst into life.

POWERING UP

Before you throw the power switch, ensure that the monitor is switched on and that there are no disks in any of the media drives – that can mean floppies, CD-ROMs, Zips or any other type of storage disk. Now turn on your PC's power switch. After a few seconds Windows 98 will start to "boot" (a techie's term for starting up the operating system). The first thing you will see is the Windows 98 main screen. This will be followed shortly by a box that asks you for a user name and password.

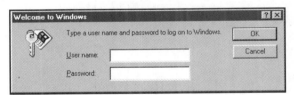

Don't panic! Since you don't yet have a user name or password you can just click on <u>OK</u> or <u>CANCEL</u> to enter Windows 98.

RUNNING WINDOWS 98 FOR THE FIRST TIME ▫▢✕

The first time you launch a new version of Windows 98 (or whenever you enter without a user name or password) you should also be greeted by a noisy and colourful little introduction which then settles down to show a box with three options: REGISTER NOW; DISCOVER WINDOWS 98; and TUNE UP YOUR COMPUTER. The first option installs a potentially useful Web link called WINDOWS UPDATE. This is an Internet site to which you can link to get new (or corrected) versions of some of Windows 98's functions as they arise. Unless you are feeling particularly confident, you might be better off leaving this until later, seeing as it requires a modem or Internet connection to work. The second option – DISCOVER WINDOWS 98 – is a multimedia tour of some of the main Windows functions, which is ideal for beginners.

THE DESKTOP

This is where much of the activity happens – the
Desktop. When you run Windows 98, the Desktop
becomes home to the various functions by which you
can interact with your PC.

DESKTOP ELEMENTS

The Desktop is made up from two essential parts – the active
area which takes up most of the screen, and the Taskbar along
the bottom. You interact with your PC by double-clicking on
the "icons". Here is a typical Desktop. Don't worry if yours
doesn't look exactly the same. This is because customized icons
have been added to the Desktop and the Taskbar since
Windows 98 was first installed

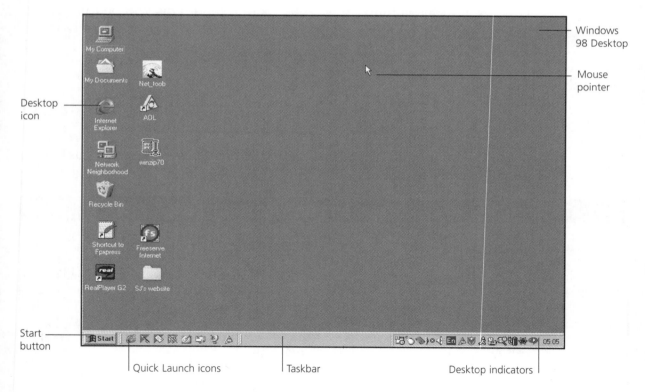

Windows
98 Desktop

Mouse
pointer

Desktop
icon

Start
button

Quick Launch icons   Taskbar   Desktop indicators

Here is a brief description of the various elements shown across the page:

WINDOWS 98 DESKTOP

The Desktop area covers the entire screen from the top down to the Taskbar. Like a "real" desktop, this is the area in which you do most of your work.

DESKTOP ICON

Every one of the "loose" assorted images you find on your Desktop is an icon. These represent the entry points to either a program, a document or a folder. For example, if you double click on the "My Documents" icon it will open up the folder of the same name, which contains assorted documents. Another possibility is that it may be a "shortcut" icon. In the example below, double-clicking on "Shortcut to Fpxpress" will launch the program FrontPage Express, but it isn't the program itself – it's just a pointer. We'll learn more about documents, folders and shortcuts in later chapters.

Folder icon

Shortcut icon

MOUSE POINTER

As you move the mouse around on your desk, the mouse pointer moves around on your desktop. It normally appears as arrow, but in different circumstances it can be shown variously as a line, a pointing hand, a question mark or an hour glass.

TASKBAR

As you will see, the grey area at the bottom of the screen can be set up to perform all kinds of diffrent functions – in fact, it doesn't even need to be at the bottom of the Desktop, but can be set at any of the other three edges.

OUSE MATTERS

Before we settle down to do something vaguely useful, it's important that we take a brief look at the most efficient ways we can make the mouse interact with both the keyboard and Windows 98.

HAND TO MOUSE

Don't worry if you never used a mouse before – in no time at all it will becomes second nature. Most right-handed people, use both hands for typing on the keyboard, but the right hand also shifts between the keyboard and navigating with the mouse. It's fairly standard to hold the mouse loosely between the thumb and third finger. This leaves the first and second fingers free to click on the buttons.

You should always use your mouse on a flat, clean surface – specially made mouse mats with a hard plastic surface and soft foam underside are ideal.

THE BUTTONS

Although mice come in a variety of styles, Windows 98 is especially geared towards those with two buttons. The "primary" button is on the left; the "secondary" button is on the right. If you are left-handed, Windows 98 has a provision for switching the buttons around (see pages 82-85).

MOUSE MOVEMENTS

By combining the movements of the mouse with clicking or holding on either of the buttons, you can activate objects on the Desktop, move them around at will, select options from menus, draw graphics, and much more besides. With just six basic manoeuvres, you can make your mouse do just about anything short of typing in text. You certainly need to be familiar with this these movements – they are not only a necessity for Windows 98, but for any programs designed to run under this operating system.

THE SIX MOUSE MOVEMENTS

Point
This is rather like "taking aim" with your mouse. You move it around so the pointer is "touching" an object on the screen.

Click
Press and release the primary mouse button while pointing at an object on the screen.

Double-click
Press and release the primary mouse button twice in quick succession while pointing at an object on the screen.

Right-Click
Press and release the secondary mouse button while pointing at an object on the screen.

Drag (drag-and-drop)
Press and hold the primary mouse button while pointing at an object on the screen. You can then drag the object to a new location and drop it in place by releasing the mouse button.

Right-drag
As drag-and-drop only with the secondary mouse button held.

THE MOUSE AND TEXT

A confusing aspect of using a mouse for the first time is understanding that the position where the mouse is pointing on a screen has (in most cases) nothing to do with the place that text will appear if you were to start typing on the keyboard. This is because the mouse pointer is NOT the same things as the cursor. If you point and click in the middle of a text document, then the cursor is likely to move to that point: in this case, text *will* appear at this position when you start to type. When you are typing text, the mouse can be useful in correcting errors, but you need to be aware of the difference between INSERTING text and OVERWRITING text. Imagine you have the phrase "FISH OR CHIPS" in your word processor. If you point and click directly before "OR", the cursor will be positioned there. If you now type in "AND", will the phrase now read "FISH AND CHIPS"? No, because you have only inserted the new text, which now says "FISH ANDOR CHIPS". To overwrite, you must point and click in the same place as before, only this time DRAG the mouse along to the right so that the word "OR" is highlighted. If you now type in "AND", your new text will replace the highlighted text.

RUNNING YOUR FIRST PROGRAM

The functions you'll perform most often with your PC are likely to include running programs, creating or opening documents, and then saving those documents. Before we get down to the minutiae of Windows 98's workings, let's look at a simple practical example.

PROGRAMS AND DOCUMENTS

Most programs are used to make something tangible, be it a letter, a spreadsheet, a sound or an image. Anything that is created by a program can be termed a "document". Some people call them "files", but this can be ambiguous, since a file is technically speaking a grouping of related binary digits. This can also refer to the program itself. Once you have created a document you can save it, close it, re-open it and edit it.

FOLDERS AND DOCUMENTS

Documents can be stored in "folders", making your PC a kind of virtual filing cabinet. It's also possible for folders to be stored in a hierarchy of sub-folders. Here is an example of how you might store your documents.

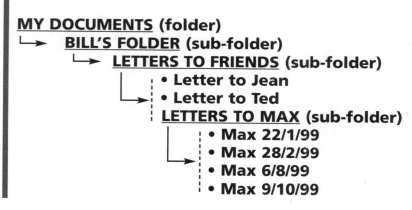

MY DOCUMENTS (folder)
→ **BILL'S FOLDER** (sub-folder)
  → **LETTERS TO FRIENDS** (sub-folder)
    • **Letter to Jean**
    • **Letter to Ted**
    LETTERS TO MAX (sub-folder)
      • **Max 22/1/99**
      • **Max 28/2/99**
      • **Max 6/8/99**
      • **Max 9/10/99**

RUNNING A PROGRAM

One of the easiest ways to open a program is to use the Start Menu, which you can launch by clicking on the Start Button. Here is a simple example that uses a VERY basic text program called NotePad that comes free with Windows 98.

1 Click on the START Button. The START MENU will appear. Move the mouse pointer to PROGRAMS.

2 Without clicking the mouse, the PROGRAMS folder will expand to a drop-down menu. Move the mouse pointer to ACCESSORIES.

3 The ACCESSORIES folder expands to a drop-down menu. Move the mouse pointer down to NOTEPAD and click.

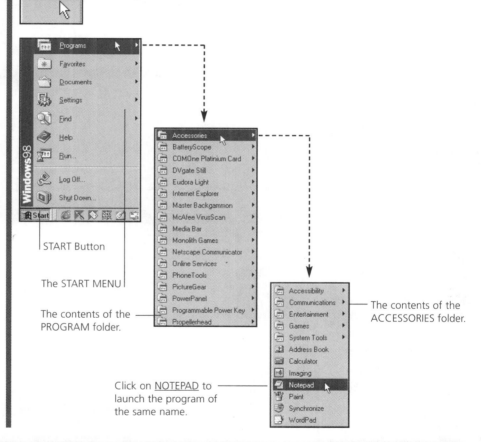

START Button

The START MENU

The contents of the PROGRAM folder.

The contents of the ACCESSORIES folder.

Click on NOTEPAD to launch the program of the same name.

RUNNING PROGRAMS

Generally speaking, when you install new programs they will be stored in the PROGRAM folder unless you specify otherwise. This is sensible practice since it keeps them all in one place – then if you want to run a program you know exactly where you can find it. For programs that you use a great deal it's a good idea to install shortcut icons on the Desktop (see page 62) or to set them up so that they can be accessed from the Start menu or Taskbar (see page 42).

CREATING A DOCUMENT

With Notepad up and running we can now get down to the serious business of creating a new document. Notepad always launches with a blank document called "Untitled" loaded.

1 The mouse pointer becomes a vertical line. This indicates that when you start typing this is where the words will appear on the screen. Now type in some text.

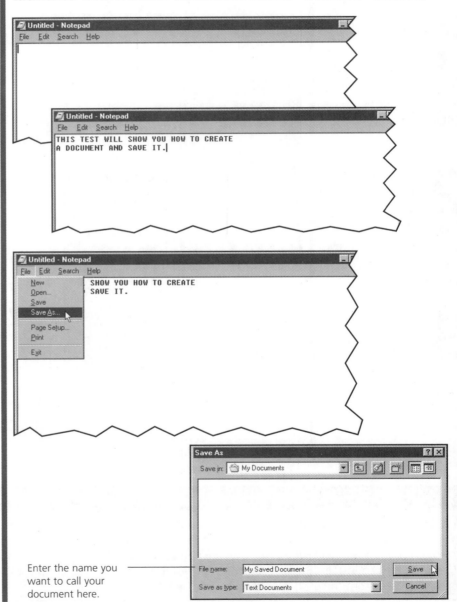

2 To save your document, place the mouse pointer over the FILE menu entry. Click and hold to see the drop-down menu. With the mouse button still held, drag the mouse down to SAVE AS and then release the button.

3 Position your mouse pointer in the FILE NAME box and click. Enter the name you want to call your document. Click on SAVE.

Enter the name you want to call your document here.

4 You can now quit the program by choosing <u>EXIT</u> from the <u>FILE</u> menu. The program will close and your document will disappear.

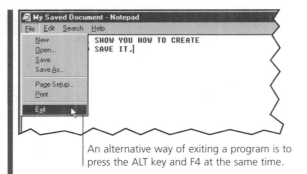

An alternative way of exiting a program is to press the ALT key and F4 at the same time.

OPENING AND EDITING A DOCUMENT

Although you have quit the Notepad program, the document you created is still on your hard disk. In this next example, we'll open the same document, edit it, and then save it again. Begin by relaunching Notepad – if you need a reminder how to do that, return to page 25 and follow steps 1 to 3.

1 Choose <u>OPEN</u> from the <u>FILE</u> menu.

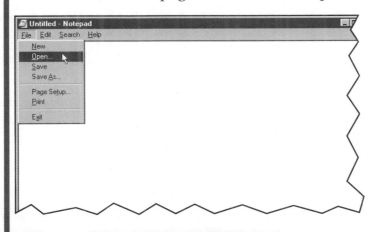

2 In the <u>OPEN</u> box, all the text files in <u>MY DOCUMENTS</u> are listed. Highlight <u>MY SAVED DOCUMENT</u> and click on <u>OPEN</u>.

3 Your original document has been reloaded. You can add to or edit the text in any way you like.

4 Save the amended document by selecting <u>SAVE AS</u> in the <u>FILE</u> menu.

5 If you don't want to overwrite your original document you can save it under a different name.

6 You can see what you have done by double-clicking on the MY DOCUMENTS icon on the Desktop. This causes the MY DOCUMENTS folder to open. As you can see, your two documents appear in the folder where you saved them.

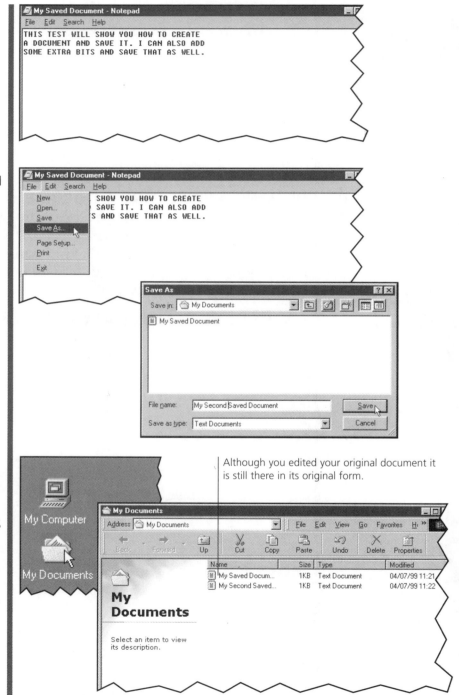

Although you edited your original document it is still there in its original form.

A SLIGHT BACKTRACK

When you re-opened your document on page 27 it was there ready and waiting for you in the "My Documents" folder. Sometimes, however, you might not know exactly where a document is located. This means that you may have to "browse" through some folders to find it. You could open My Documents and then systematically go through each folder until you find what you want, and then return to Notepad, or you can do it from within the program.

1 Click on TED'S FOLDER if you think that's where your original document might be. Click on OPEN.

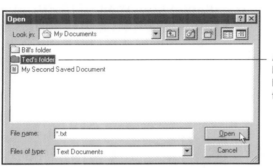

An alternative to using the OPEN button to open the folder would have been to double-click on the folder name.

2 The document is in the folder. You can open it by highlighting the document name with a click, and then clicking on OPEN.

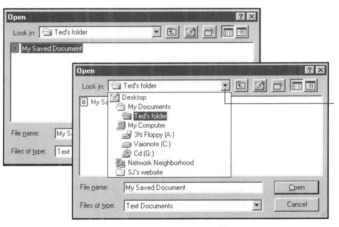

Had your document not been there you would have had to return to the "parent" folder. To do this, click on the arrow and choose My Documents. This would return the OPEN box to how it was in step 1.

A NEEDLE IN A HAYSTACK _ □ X

The example above is all well and good if you have a reasonable idea of whereabouts the document you're looking for is located. If you don't though, it could take you a considerable amount of time. Luckily, Windows 98 provides you with a very sophisticated FIND function, located in the START menu. This will be discussed on page 59.

TAKE FIVE

Although we've only just scratched the surface of Windows 98's potential, the kinds of function you've just performed cover a surprisingly large proportion of PC usage.

CLOSING WINDOWS 98

So far we've deliberately performed some basic tasks the long way round so you can see how they work. You'll soon find many shortcuts. Instead of re-opening your document from within Notepad, for example, you could simply have double-clicked on the document's icon within the folder – this would have launched Notepad with your document open in place. For now, take a break from Windows 98 – here's how to shut down.

1 Click on the START button. From the START menu, click on SHUT DOWN.

2 In the SHUT DOWN WINDOWS box, click on the SHUT DOWN button. Click on OK.

SHUT DOWN closes down Windows and switches off your PC.

RESTART closes down Windows, switches off your PC and then switches it back on again.

These switches are known as "Radio Buttons". A single click toggles between on and off, or vice versa. Only one option can be "on".

THE TRUTH ABOUT WINDOWS

2

The reason that the Windows operating system is so-named is because it makes extensive use of rectangular boxes called "windows" to display information or run programs. Windows 98 can have several of these windows open at any one time. Because of their fundamental importance, this chapter is devoted largely to the basics of navigating around and between windows.

WINDOWS IN DETAIL

Even though we haven't identified them by name, you have already come across several examples of windows in the first chapter. Let's begin with an annotated look at the features that are common to every type of window.

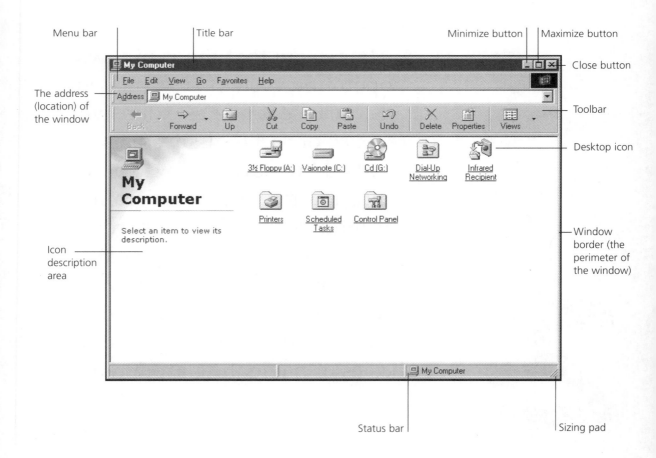

Menu bar | Title bar | Minimize button | Maximize button

Close button

The address (location) of the window

Toolbar

Desktop icon

Icon description area

Window border (the perimeter of the window)

Status bar | Sizing pad

WINDOWS AND THE TASKBAR

Each time you open a window, it also appears as a button in the taskbar at the foot of the page.

Only one button appears in the taskbar indicating that MY COMPUTER is the only window open on the Desktop.

WINDOW ELEMENTS

Here is a brief overview of some of the elements of the window shown opposite. Most of them allow you to control aspects of the window's appearance.

TITLE BAR

This shows the name of the window. Double-click anywhere in the main part of the title bar to expand the window to the full size of your PC's screen. This is called "maximizing". Double-click again to reduce the window to its former size and position. It's also possible to move the window around by clicking and holding on the title bar.

1 Click and hold on the title bar. Drag the window and release the mouse button at the new location.

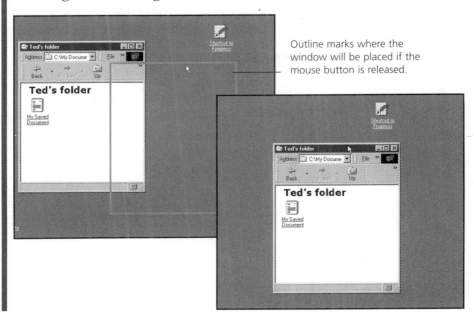

Outline marks where the window will be placed if the mouse button is released.

CLOSE BUTTON

Closes the window.

MAXIMIZE AND MINIMIZE BUTTONS

Clicking on the Maximize button is similar to double-clicking on the Title bar. Clicking on the Minimize button gives the appearance of closing the window, but in fact reduces it to a button on the Taskbar at the foot of the screen. If you click on the Taskbar button it will restore the window to the Desktop.

MENU BAR

The Menu bar contains options which are relevant to the program running inside the window. Clicking on any of the Menu bar headings generates a drop-down list from which you can select a variety of functions. Although each menu will differ from program to program, designers have sought to maintain a degree of uniformity. Menu bars will be covered in greater depth in Chapter 3.

WINDOW BORDER

You can drag the border at any point to change the size and shape of the window. Dragging the horizontal borders alters the height; dragging the vertical borders alters the width.

1 Click and hold on the border. Drag the border and release the mouse button to create a new perimeter.

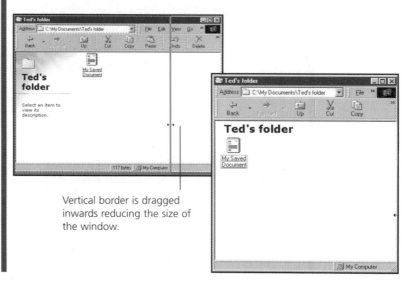

Vertical border is dragged inwards reducing the size of the window.

TOOLBAR

The toolbar contains shortcut buttons to some of the commonly used menu bar functions.

VIEW menu options

GO menu options   EDIT menu options   FILE menu options

SIZING PAD

Drag the corner of the window to resize on both the horizontal and vertical axes.

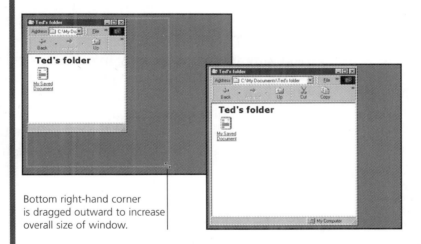

Bottom right-hand corner is dragged outward to increase overall size of window.

ICON DESCRIPTION

If you rest the mouse over an icon, descriptive information appears on the left of the screen.

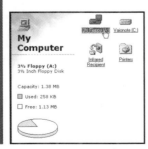

A CHOICE OF VIEWING

After the hype that surrounded the launch of Windows 95 a few years ago, many were less than enthralled at the prospect of upgrading to the newer version. In fact, the main difference between Windows 95 and its newer sibling is in the options for viewing windows.

INTERNET INFLUENCE

Realizing that a whole new market was being turned on to personal computing by the growing appeal of the Internet, Microsoft introduced Windows 98 so that windows could optionally be displayed as if they were Web pages. Although this has not been a radical advance in functionality, it does make working on your PC appear a more friendly proposition.

CLASSIC VERSUS THE WEB

As a Windows 98 user, you have a choice in the way they you can now view windows. You can opt for the "classic" traditional window, the new "Web" window, or you can mix and match the two. Those used to older versions of Windows should be aware that a new approach to navigating is needed if you go with Web-style viewing. In an effort to make the experience of using Windows 98 as simple as surfing the World Wide Web, navigation in this mode only requires a single click – the mouse pointer turning into a finger icon like a Web browser poised over a hyperlink. In the "classic" mode you have to double-click on an icon to make it do anything.

Throughout the book we'll mostly use the new Web-style windows. For now, however, let's take a look at the two approaches side by side.

SETTING THE STYLE

The next examples will show you how to set the viewing style for both classic and Web mode.

1 Click the START button.

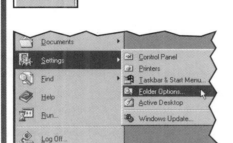

2 From the START menu select SETTINGS and then FOLDER OPTIONS.

3 In the FOLDERS OPTIONS window, click on WEB STYLE. Click on OK. Your windows will now appear "Web-style".

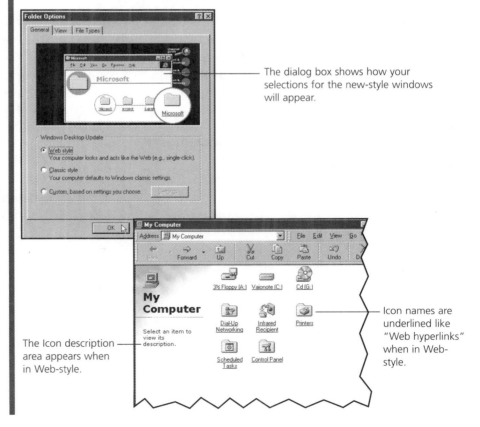

The dialog box shows how your selections for the new-style windows will appear.

Icon names are underlined like "Web hyperlinks" when in Web-style.

The Icon description area appears when in Web-style.

4 To set up your windows in the "classic" style, repeat steps 1 and 2. In the <u>FOLDERS OPTIONS</u> window, click on <u>CLASSIC STYLE</u>. Click on <u>OK</u>. Your windows will now appear "classic style".

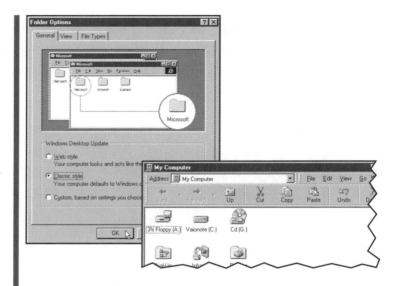

THE HYBRID APPROACH

On balance, the "classic" window would seem to have little to commend it over the "Web style". Some, however, may find that the descriptive area of the Web-style window is a waste of space, even if they like being able to navigate with a single click of the mouse button. The Custom Settings dialog box enables you to mix and match between the two styles.

1 In <u>FOLDER OPTIONS</u>, click on <u>CUSTOM</u> and then on <u>SETTINGS</u> click on <u>OK</u>.

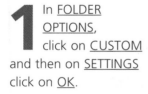

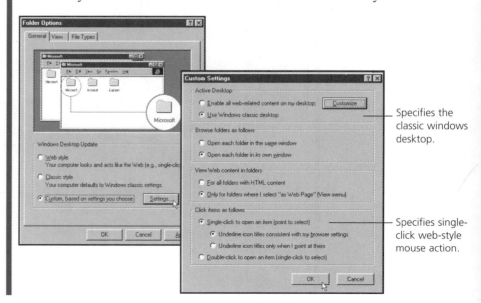

Specifies the classic windows desktop.

Specifies single-click web-style mouse action.

CROLL BARS

You can alter the size of your window as much as you like, but it won't affect the number of documents or programs inside. What may happen, however, is that you won't be able to see them all at the same time. You can access these "hidden" parts of the window by using "scroll bars"

HOW CAN YOU TELL THERE'S MORE?

You can tell when a window holds more than is currently being displayed when grey sliders with arrows at either end appear on the right and/or bottom of the window. These are scroll bars. There are two ways to use scroll bars: you can either click on the scrolling arrows to move up, down or across, or you can drag the scroll blocks using the mouse.

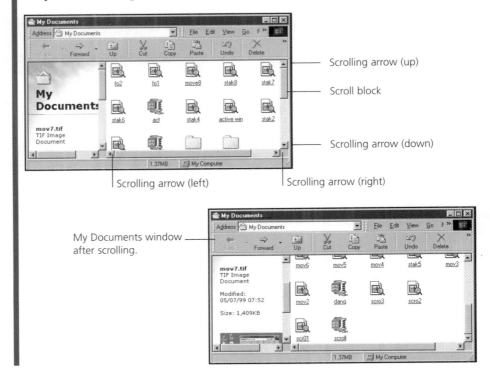

Scrolling arrow (up)

Scroll block

Scrolling arrow (down)

Scrolling arrow (left)

Scrolling arrow (right)

My Documents window after scrolling.

ACTIVE WINDOWS

You can have a large number of windows open on your Desktop at any given time. Indeed, you're only really limited by how much RAM your PC has at its disposal. But however many windows are open, only one at a time can be "active".

HOW CAN YOU TELL WHICH IS ACTIVE?

If you think of all the windows you currently have open on your Desktop as being in a huge pile, the one sitting at the very top is the "active" window. This means that whatever you happen to be doing with your keyboard or mouse, it will only have an impact on that one window. There are two ways in which you can tell immediately whether a window is active:

- The title bar is shown in colour when active.

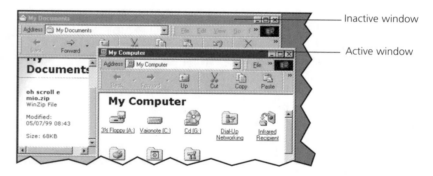

Inactive window

Active window

- The active window's taskbar button looks as if it's been pressed in.

Inactive window   Active window

MAKING A WINDOW ACTIVE

For you to type text into a window, or add anything else using your keyboard or mouse, it has to be active. It's true that there are certain functions, such as Internet downloads, that can trundle away on their own inside an inactive window. This is known as running in the "background". But even then, it isn't possible for you to intervene personally without making that window active.

There are several other ways of making a window active when a number of them are open on your Desktop.

- Click on any part of the window in the Desktop.
- Click on the window's button in the taskbar.
- Keep pressing the <u>Alt</u> key and the <u>Esc</u> key together until the desired window becomes active.
- Press the <u>Alt</u> key and the <u>Tab</u> key. This displays a series of icons that each represent a window in a panel at the centre of the screen. Press the keys until you stop at the window you wish to make active. This is useful if you have a lot of windows open.

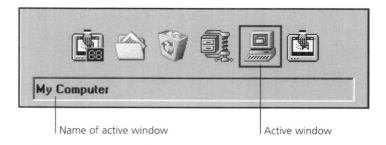

Name of active window   Active window

ACTIVATING HIDDEN WINDOWS

If you have clicked on a window's Minimize button (see page 34) you will see that there is no presence on the Desktop. Nonetheless, because you haven't clicked on the Close button (see also page 34), the window remains open but hidden from the Desktop. The only clue you have of its existence is that the window still has a button in the Taskbar. By clicking on this button you will not only restore the window on the desktop but also make it the active window. It's always a good idea to keep your eye on the Taskbar – when you are using the <u>Alt+Esc</u> or <u>Alt+Tab</u> toggling techniques shown above, the sequence in which each window is activated is the same as they appear in the taskbar. Even if a window has been minimized, the taskbar button will still illuminate while you are shuffling through each open window.

ARRANGING WINDOWS

A problem of having too many windows open at any one time is that your Desktop can easily become a confused muddle. Luckily, Windows 98 has several useful features that will enable you to continue to work with multiple windows and keep your Desktop reasonably well organized.

CASCADING WINDOWS

You can easily turn a messy Desktop like the one shown below into a neat cascade of easily accessible windows.

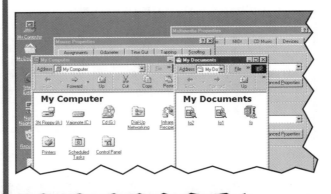

1 Right-click on any empty space along the taskbar.

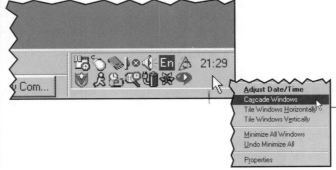

2 From the pop-up menu that appears, select CASCADE WINDOWS.

3 The windows on the Desktop are neatly arranged in a cascade.

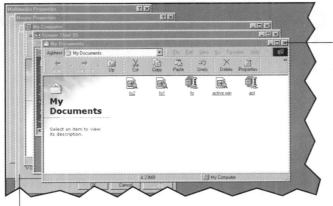

The windows are displayed so that each title bar can be read easily.

Click anywhere on any window to make it active (and bring it to the front).

TILING WINDOWS

You can also arrange windows so that they are "tiled". This means that the windows are resized so that they appear to fill up the Desktop.

1 Right-click on any empty space along the taskbar. Select TILE WINDOWS HORIZONTALLY from the pop-up menu.

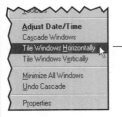

With more than two windows open, it doesn't matter which tiling option you choose. With two windows, horizontal tiling fits them into the Desktop one above the other; vertical tiling fits them side by side.

2 The windows on the Desktop are neatly tiled.

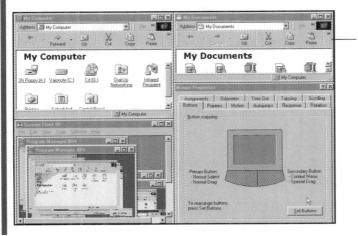

Click on any window to make it active.

MOVING ICONS

We'll finish this chapter with a look at the way you can move icons around within your windows. As you will see later, these principles are also used when you copy documents.

REARRANGING WINDOWS

You can reposition the icons in any window simply by using the drag and drop technique.

1 Click and hold on the icon you wish to move. Drag the icon to the new position and release the mouse button.

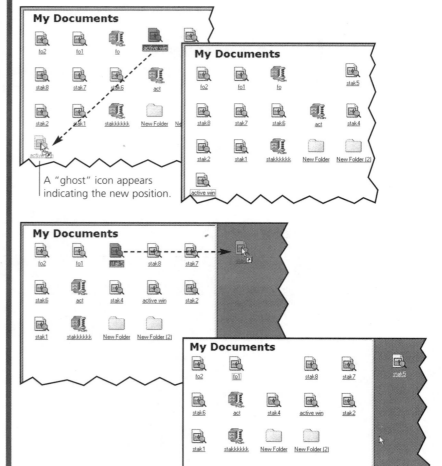

A "ghost" icon appears indicating the new position.

2 The same method can be used to drag icons from a window to the desktop or into a folder.

WHAT'S ON THE MENU?

3

The system of selecting options from a series of menus is at the very heart of the way most of us use our PCs. The principal functions of every program written to run under a Windows 98 operating system are built into these menus. Although the header options are largely the same, the contents of each menu are tailored strictly to the needs of the program.

ENU OPTIONS

Each window has its own sets of menus just beneath the title bar. These contain groups of commands in drop-down lists. You can access each set of options by clicking on the menu header, dragging through the list and releasing the mouse button on the required option. Most windows have the same set of headers but contain specific options that are unique their own functions.

MENU OPTIONS

When you select an option from a menu there are a number of possible outcomes. You may execute a simple function, such as COPY, CUT or PASTE; you may select options from a list; you may tick "on-off" switches; a further drop-down menu may result; or, for more complex functions, you may have to configure settings in a dialog box.

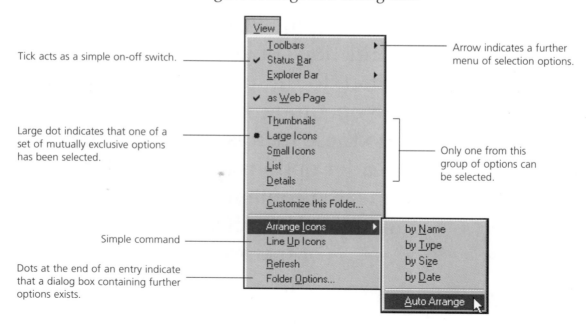

Tick acts as a simple on-off switch.

Arrow indicates a further menu of selection options.

Large dot indicates that one of a set of mutually exclusive options has been selected.

Only one from this group of options can be selected.

Simple command

Dots at the end of an entry indicate that a dialog box containing further options exists.

COPY AND PASTE

Two of the most fundamental options for all PC users can be found in the <u>EDIT</u> menus of most programs. They are <u>COPY</u> and <u>PASTE</u>. These commands allow you to move or copy information between windows programs (or within the same program) using a temporary storage area called the "clipboard". The example below shows a scan which has been modified using the Windows 98 Paint program (see pages 98-99), copied into the clipboard and pasted into WordPad (see pages 94-96).

1 In <u>PAINT</u>, use the area tool to highlight the image to be copied. Choose <u>COPY</u> from the <u>EDIT</u> menu.

Area to be copied to the clipboard.

2 Open an untitled document in <u>WORDPAD.</u> Choose <u>PASTE</u> from the <u>EDIT</u> menu. The image is pasted into place.

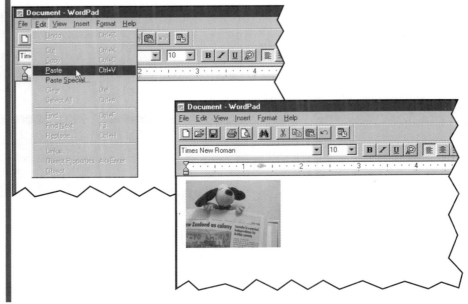

IALOG BOXES

Some functions require far more detailed settings than can be chosen from a simple drop-down menu. In such cases, a new window will open up with the capability of addressing a more complex set of options. These windows are called "dialog boxes".

DIALOG BOXES

No two dialog boxes look alike. This is because they are designed to perform an extremely limited but specific set of tasks. Dialog boxes are designed to be used with the mouse, only ever needing keyboard input when it becomes necessary to enter text. All dialog boxes are made up from broadly the same set of components. Conventions for the design of dialog box have evolved so that the elements look like everyday items, such as radio dials. We'll take a look at the possible functions within a dialog box over the next few pages.

TABS

Where there is too much information to get into a single box, the options are split into a number of "tab" pages. This takes its idea from desk filing systems and the marker tabs that identify the contents within the files. Click on the tab to change to a new set of options.

Screen associated with the buttons tab.

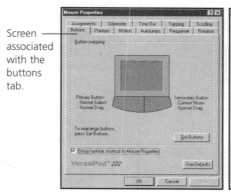

Screen associated with the pointer tab.

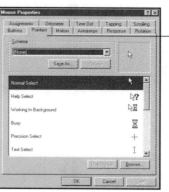

BUTTONS

Most boxes have at least three buttons, the most common being "OK", "Cancel" and "Apply". To activate a button you simply click on it.

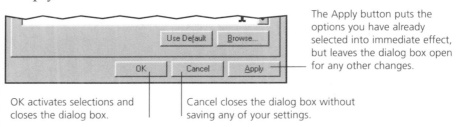

The Apply button puts the options you have already selected into immediate effect, but leaves the dialog box open for any other changes.

OK activates selections and closes the dialog box.

Cancel closes the dialog box without saving any of your settings.

TITLE BAR BOXES

Just like other windows, the "cross" at the top right-hand corner of a dialog box closes it, and has the same effect as the Cancel button. Some dialog boxes also have a Help button. If you click on the Help button, the mouse pointer changes to a question mark. You can click the pointer on any areas of the dialog box to get assistance.

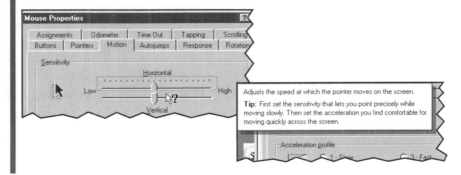

ONLINE HELP

Windows 98 has a particularly sophisticated in-built online help facility. You can access it by selecting HELP from the START MENU. The main window has three option tabs: a list of help topics ("Exploring Your Computer", for example); Index of topics (in alphabetical order); or a keyword search. Particularly useful are the Windows 98 Troubleshooters. Select an aspect of Windows that's causing a problem and the troubleshooter asks you a series of "true or false" questions. Based on how you respond the Troubleshooter will endeavour to come up with possible solutions.

OPTION BUTTONS

Sometimes called "radio buttons", option buttons present an array of mutually exclusive options. Clicking on a blank button will switch it on and switch off the previous choice.

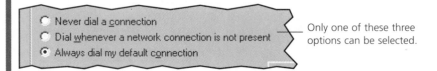

Only one of these three options can be selected.

TICK BOXES

Sometimes called "check boxes", if you click on one of these a tick will appear in the box; click again and it will vanish. Tick boxes are simply a list of possible options – you can tick any number of them, or none at all.

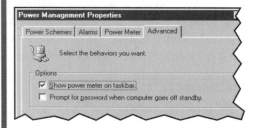

SLIDERS

A slider is used to allow the user to select a position between two points, like a volume control, for example, which can be set at any position between no sound and maximum loudness. To move the slider, place the mouse pointer over the "knob" and drag in the appropriate direction.

DROP-DOWN LISTS

Drop-down lists are a fundamental part of life for most PC users. They crop up all over the place. A drop-down list appears to be a box containing a single line of text with a downward-pointing arrow alongside. When you click on the arrow, a list of choices "drops down" beneath the text box. If there are a large number of choices, you may even have to use a scroll bar to see all of the options.

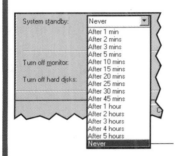

Your choice from the drop-down list appears in the box at the top. Only this remains when the list disappears.

LIST BOXES

Rather like drop-down lists, list boxes are simply a selection of options from which you choose. They are often accessed by scroll bars, and in some cases can allow for multiple choices to be made.

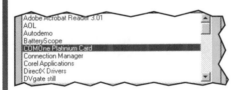

SPIN BUTTONS

Sometimes you will encounter a numerical text box with a pair of arrows alongside. This is a spin button. Clicking the "up" arrow increments the number; clicking the "down" arrow decrements the number.

Click on arrows to change the number.

KEYBOARD SHORTCUTS

One of the neatest things about Windows is the way it's possible to navigate through the menu system without using the mouse. This is possible by taking keyboard shortcuts. Once you've learned how the codes operate you can work much faster on your PC.

WATCH THE UNDERLINING

You may have noticed while you were looking at the different menus that pretty well every entry has an underlined letter. This is to allow you to make keyboard shortcuts. The rule is a relatively simple one. To access the drop-down menu you must hold the ALT key and press the underlined letter: ALT+V will open the View Menu. With the menu opened out, press any underlined letter to launch the command: press T to open the Toolbar sub-menu. It's as simple as that.

1 Press ALT+V to open the VIEW MENU.

2 Press T to open the TOOLBARS sub-menu.

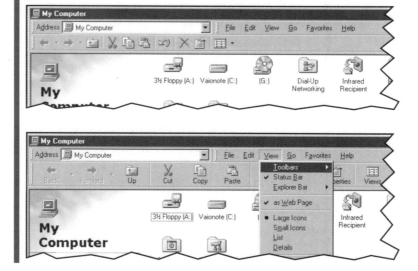

3 Press T to switch off the TEXT LABELS option.

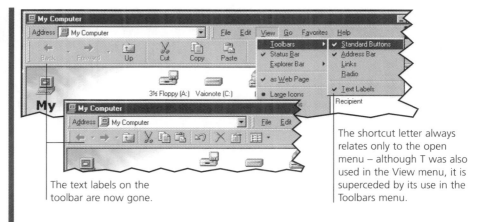

The shortcut letter always relates only to the open menu – although T was also used in the View menu, it is superceded by its use in the Toolbars menu.

The text labels on the toolbar are now gone.

DON'T TOUCH THAT MOUSE

This little exercise will show you how it's possible to move from the Desktop to opening a specific document in a specific folder by just using keystrokes.

1 Highlight the MY DOCUMENTS, folder. Press the ENTER key.

If one of the items on the Desktop is highlighted you can navigate through the other items by using the directional arrows on the keyboard.

2 Press the TAB key to highlight one of the documents in the folder. Use the directional arrows to get to the document you require. Press ALT+F to open the FILE MENU and then O to OPEN the document.

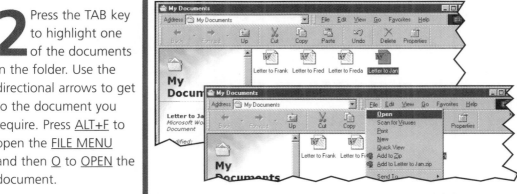

3 OPEN launches the program with the document loaded.

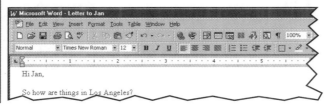

SHORTCUT ICONS

You can use shortcut icons to give you immediate access to programs and folders that you use often. Instead of having to navigate through layers of folders you simply click on an icon.

ADDING A SHORTCUT

In this example we'll dig deeply into the Program Files folder to find Microsoft FrontPage Express and create a shortcut so that the program can be launched from the Desktop.

1 Right-click and hold on the icon. Drag out of the window and release the mouse button. A drop-down menu appears. Click on <u>CREATE SHORT-CUT(S) HERE</u>.

2 You can launch the program by double-clicking on the shortcut icon. If you ever want to delete the shortcut, simply drag it into the Recycle Bin – the original program will not be harmed in any way.

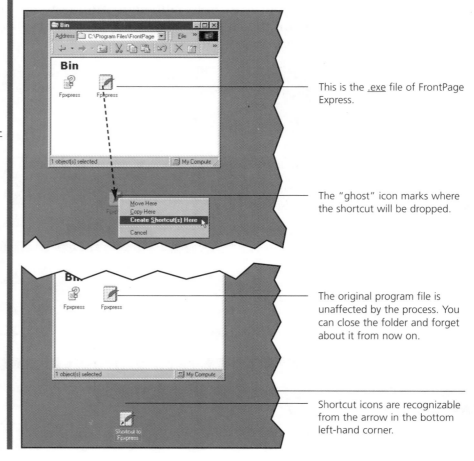

This is the <u>.exe</u> file of FrontPage Express.

The "ghost" icon marks where the shortcut will be dropped.

The original program file is unaffected by the process. You can close the folder and forget about it from now on.

Shortcut icons are recognizable from the arrow in the bottom left-hand corner.

FILES AND FOLDERS

4

Windows 98 is geared
completely towards allowing
you to work efficiently.
A crucial factor is the way
in which you organize your
documents within folders. This
chapter introduces the Windows
Explorer, a program that gives
you an at-a-glance overview of
your work and allows you to
move documents quickly and
simply between folders.

WINDOWS EXPLORER

Windows Explorer is a handy program which allows you to view your documents, folders and "file paths" (the hierarchy of folders and sub-folders). You can also use it to move, rename and delete documents. You can find Windows Explorer in the Start Menu's Program folder.

1 Click on <u>START</u>. Choose <u>PROGRAM</u> from the <u>START MENU</u>, and <u>WINDOWS EXPLORER</u> from the drop-down list.

Windows Explorer's left-hand panel contains your PC's folder hierarchy.

The "Minus box" shows the files or sub-folders within.

Click on a "plus" box to collapse the folder, making its contents visible.

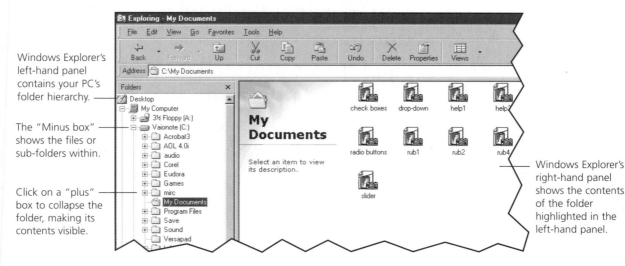

Windows Explorer's right-hand panel shows the contents of the folder highlighted in the left-hand panel.

MOVING FILES IN WINDOWS EXPLORER

The great benefit of working with Windows Explorer is that all of your folders and their contents are easily accessible from one screen. Not only does this make viewing the contents of folders more straightforward, but you can also perform the same kinds of actions on documents as you can from within a window. Here is an example of moving a series of files from one folder to another.

1 Click on MY DOCUMENTS in the FOLDERS list. The contents of the folder appear in the right-hand panel. Drag out a box to highlight the documents you want to move.

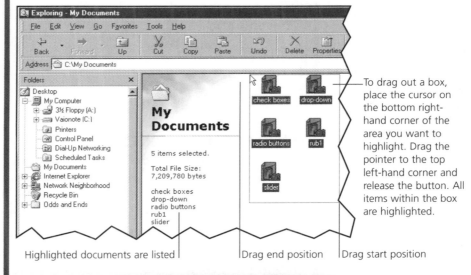

To drag out a box, place the cursor on the bottom right-hand corner of the area you want to highlight. Drag the pointer to the top left-hand corner and release the button. All items within the box are highlighted.

Highlighted documents are listed | Drag end position | Drag start position

2 Drag and drop the highlighted files in the right-hand panel into ODDS AND ENDS in the folder panel.

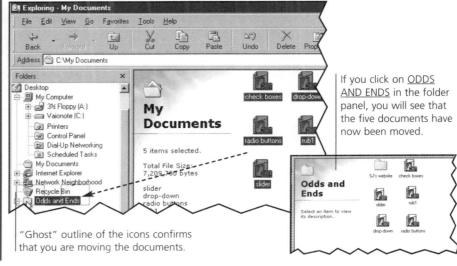

If you click on ODDS AND ENDS in the folder panel, you will see that the five documents have now been moved.

"Ghost" outline of the icons confirms that you are moving the documents.

MOVING NON-ADJACENT DOCUMENTS

Dragging out a box to highlight documents to be copied is handy way of moving things around, but it only works when the contents can be readily "enveloped". For this to be possible they all have to be grouped together. But you can also drag-and-drop non-adjacent items.

1 Click on the first document you want to move. Now hold down the CONTROL key and click on the next. You can do this as many times as you want.

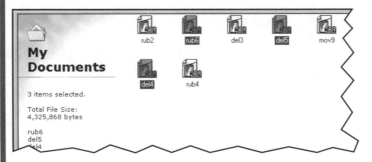

DESELECTING CHOICES

You can also deselect documents you have chosen by using "control and click" on a highlighted document. If you want to move the entire contents of a large folder except for one or two documents, you can integrate both methods, by dragging a box to cover all the documents in the folder (or you could shortcut this with a "select all" – CTL+A) and then control clicking to deselect those you don't want to copy.

1 Drag out a box to highlight the outer limits of the the selection you want to move. Holding down the CONTROL KEY, click on any documents from the selection that you do NOT want to move.

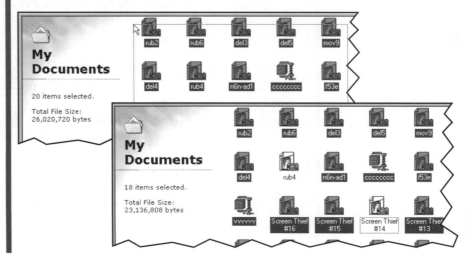

FINDING FILES

It's easy to lose track of the files on your PC - there are just so many of them. Luckily, Windows 98 has a very powerful search tool that can find missing files for you based on keywords that you provide.

1 Click on START. Choose FIND in the START MENU. Select FILES OR FOLDERS from the drop-down menu

2 The FIND ALL FILES dialog box opens. Click on the NAME & LOCATION tab. Enter your keyword and click on FIND NOW. If the search yields results they appear in a scrolling list at the foot of the dialog box.

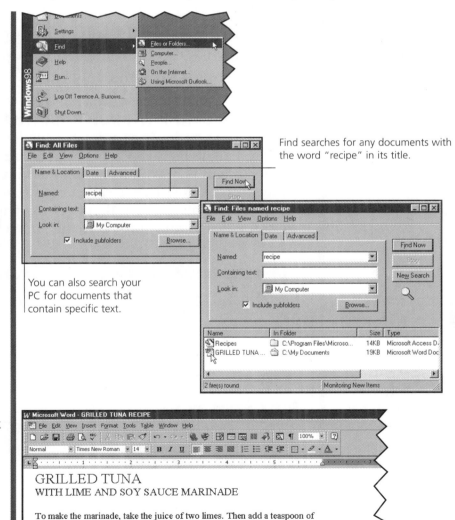

Find searches for any documents with the word "recipe" in its title.

You can also search your PC for documents that contain specific text.

3 If you double-click on the document in the scroll bar, it opens up.

DELETING YOUR DOCUMENTS

Many of the documents that you create or read on your PC are clearly not intended to stay there forever – if they did you would soon run out of space on your hard disk. So there has to be a way of getting rid of files that you no longer want.

WHAT DO WE DO WITH OUR RUBBISH?

Almost every window has a delete function, which can be found in the File menu. Whenever you you use this command, your document is moved from its folder into a special folder for unwanted items. This is called the Recycle Bin. You can find out a little more about that over the page. For now let's look at the delete functions. Once again, we'll use Windows Explorer to help out.

1 Select a folder that contains documents you want to delete. Drag out a box to highlight the documents (or choose them with "control plus click" if you would prefer).

2 Click on the FILE menu.

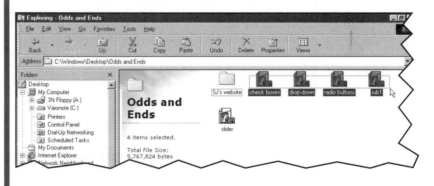

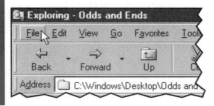

3 From the FILE menu, click on DELETE.

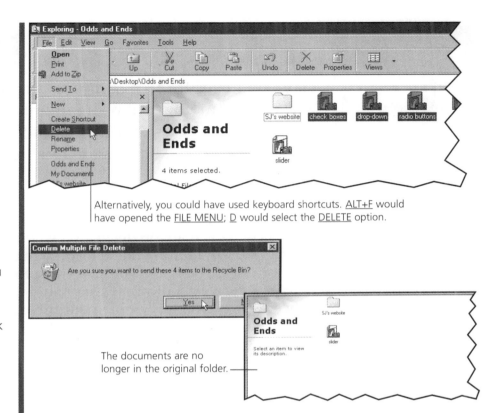

Alternatively, you could have used keyboard shortcuts. ALT+F would have opened the FILE MENU; D would select the DELETE option.

4 A small dialog box will ask you to confirm that you want to go ahead with the deletion. Click on YES.

The documents are no longer in the original folder.

DRAG THEM IN THE BIN

An alternative to using the menu options would have been simply to highlight the files and then drag-and-drop them into the Recycle Bin.

1 Drag out a box to highlight the documents you want to move. Drag your selection to the RECYCLE BIN and release the mouse button.

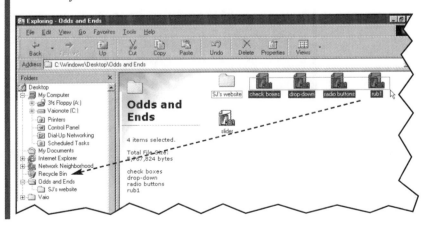

THE RECYCLE BIN

Have you ever thrown something that you thought was useless in your rubbish bin only to regret it later? Windows 98 knows that this kind of thing happens all the time and so equips the Desktop with its own Recycle Bin.

WHEN DOES RUBBISH LEAVE THE HARD DISK?

Any documents that you delete in the normal way are not actually erased, they are merely stored in the Recycle Bin. They can easily be retrieved by opening the Recycle Bin and dragging them out onto the Desktop or into a folder. They are only erased when you "empty your rubbish", by performing the deletion from within the Recycle Bin.

1 Double-click on the <u>RECYCLE BIN</u> icon. To recover an item from the Recycle Bin, drag-and-drop onto the Desktop (or into a folder).

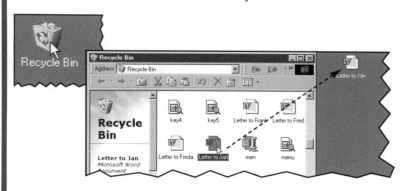

2 To permanently delete the files that remain, choose <u>EMPTY RECYCLE BIN</u>, in the <u>FILE</u> menu. A window will ask you to confirm that you really want to delete them all. Click on <u>YES</u>.

WORKING SMARTER

5

As you've already seen, Windows offers you numerous ways of doing the same tasks. Whichever you choose will depend on your own preferred ways of working. You should, however, take a careful look at the potential for customizing the Start menu and Taskbars. Many users leave them with their default settings simply because they don't know better. In fact, they can be configured to help you work more efficiently and to maintain an organized Desktop

WORKING WITH THE TASKBAR

You've already come into contact with the Taskbar that stretches along the edge of the Desktop. To begin with, it houses the all-important Windows 98 Start button. You've also seen how it indicates which of your windows are currently open. Over the next few pages we'll look at other Taskbar functions, and how you can customize it to your own preferences.

WHAT IS THE TASKBAR

This is the bar that stretches along the edge of the Desktop. Among other possibilities, the Taskbar contains the Start button that triggers the Start menu, a variety of program launch icons and indicators, and the open windows buttons. The different aspects of the Taskbar can be grouped together and viewed as toolbars in their own right. For example, the icons next to the Start Button are collectively known as the Quick Launch toolbar.

The great thing about the toolbar is that it lets you launch programs with a double-click of an icon instead of having to manoeuvre through sets of menus or setting up shortcuts that clog up your Desktop. Here are some of the main components of the Taskbar.

Each icon launches a program.

Each button represents an open window.

| Start | Screen... | WinZip... | My Co... | 11:50 |

Start button that launches the Start menu.

Quick launch toolbar

Indicators of Control Panel functions

TASKBAR PRIORITIES

Under normal circumstances the Taskbar will remain visible whatever is happening on the Desktop. However, you can make a number of basic changes by selecting from the Taskbar Properties dialog box. To call up this screen, right-click on any neutral part of the taskbar – that means anywhere on the panel that isn't an active button.

1 Select PROPERTIES from the pop-up menu.

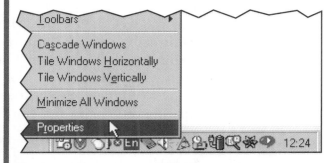

2 In the TASKBAR PROPERTIES dialog box, click on the TASKBAR OPTIONS tab. Tick the options as required. Click on OK.

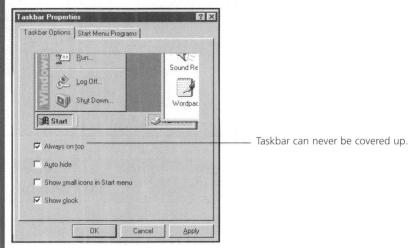

Taskbar can never be covered up.

The configuration shown above represents a good safe bet for most situations. If you tick AUTO HIDE, this turns the Taskbar into a narrow grey strip which is just visible at the foot of the desktop. To restore the Taskbar temporarily you have to rest the mouse pointer on the grey strip.

Not surprisingly, the SHOW CLOCK option displays the time in the bottom right-hand corner of the Taskbar.

TOOLBARS AVAILABLE

The Taskbar has four dedicated toolbars available. Only one of them is set up by default – that's the Quick Launch toolbar. The three others are the Desktop toolbar, Address toolbar and Links toolbar. The Desktop toolbar provides a button for every icon you have on your Desktop. Although this may not sound terribly useful at first, when you see it in action you'll see its merits. The Address and Links toolbars are only really useful if the Internet is central to your PC life. They allow you to type in Web addresses directly, or click on links that you've saved as "Favorites" within Internet Explorer. You can find out more about the Internet in Chapter 9.

Now let's see how to change the Taskbar's toolbar options. Begin by right-clicking on a neutral area of the Taskbar.

1 Select <u>TOOLBARS</u> from the pop-up menu. Select <u>DESKTOP</u> to activate the Desktop toolbar.

2 The Desktop toolbar appears in the Taskbar.

Click on My Computer to open window.

Click on arrows for pop-up menu of other icons on the Desktop.

3 You can tidy up the Taskbar by holding the cursor over the toolbar borders and dragging them to a new position.

The horizontal double-ended arrow shows that you can now drag the border.

4 The area allocated for the Desktop toolbar now only has sufficient room for the name and the double arrow icon. To see (or select) the contents of the Desktop, click on the double arrow.

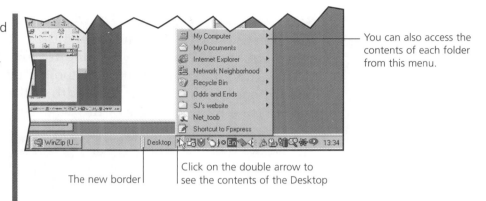

You can also access the contents of each folder from this menu.

The new border

Click on the double arrow to see the contents of the Desktop

CHANGING TOOLBAR APPEARANCES

You can also alter the way various visual characteristics of the toolbars appear. Each toolbar has a slightly different set of options.

1 To access the options for each menu, right-click on the border line to the left of each toolbar.

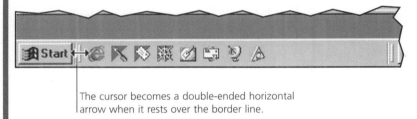

The cursor becomes a double-ended horizontal arrow when it rests over the border line.

2 In the pop-up menu select <u>VIEW</u> and then <u>LARGE</u>.

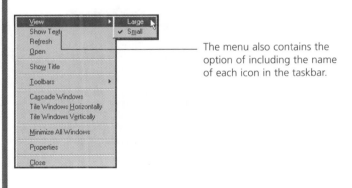

The menu also contains the option of including the name of each icon in the taskbar.

3 The Taskbar doubles its width to accommodate the new full-size launch icons.

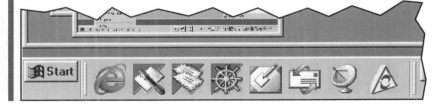

SIZE AND POSITION OF THE TASKBAR

Just because the Taskbar appears at the bottom of the Desktop when you load Windows 98, it doesn't mean that you have to do the same thing. In addition to toolbar changes you've already seen, you can alter the width of the taskbar, or even move it to a different edge of the desktop.

1 To change the width of the taskbar, position the mouse on the inner edge, click, drag and release at the new width.

2 The toolbars automatically adjust their positions.

3 To move the entire taskbar, click and hold on a neutral position within the bar. Drag the "ghost" outline of the taskbar to a new position and release the mouse button.

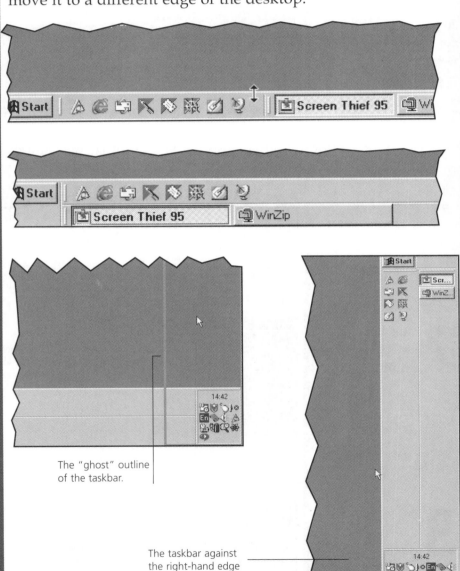

The "ghost" outline of the taskbar.

The taskbar against the right-hand edge of the Desktop.

4 You can further improve the appearance of your new Taskbar by increasing the size of the Quick Launch toolbar (see page 71).

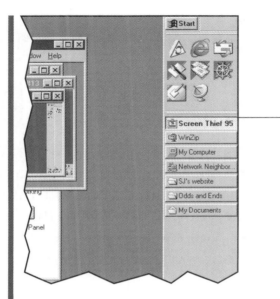

The open windows line up neatly in the new vertical taskbar.

ADDING TO THE QUICK LAUNCH TOOLBAR

Using the Quick Launch menu to run your programs is a much neater option than cluttering up your screen with the shortcut icons you learned about in Chapter 3. This is how easy it is to convert a shortcut into a Quick Launch icon.

1 Click on the shortcut you wish to move. Drag and drop it in a neutral spot in the Quick Launch toolbar.

2 The icon is now in the Quick Launch toolbar. You can delete the original Desktop shortcut by dragging and dropping it into the Recycle Bin.

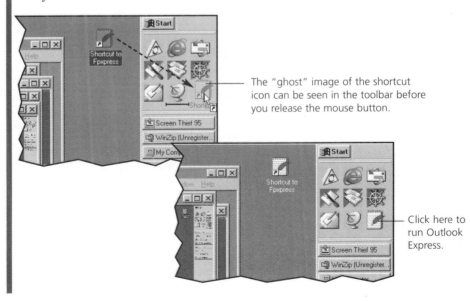

The "ghost" image of the shortcut icon can be seen in the toolbar before you release the mouse button.

Click here to run Outlook Express.

CUSTOMIZING THE START MENU

The Start menu contains the basic program and document shortcuts you need to navigate around your PC. You can find your software in the Programs folder and your documents in the Documents folder. However, you can also personalize the Start menu, adding your own essential shortcuts to programs, folders and documents.

ADDING TO THE START MENU

The basic components of the Windows 98 Start Menu are shown on the right. You may even find that your version has more entries than that. There are several different ways in which you can add your own menu entries. Two methods are shown here.

1 Right-click on the <u>START BUTTON</u>. This opens the <u>START MENU</u> window.

2 Click on a folder on the Desktop. Drag and drop inside the <u>START MENU</u> window. That folder can now be accessed from the Start menu.

The folder now appears in the Start menu. Its contents are listed alongside.

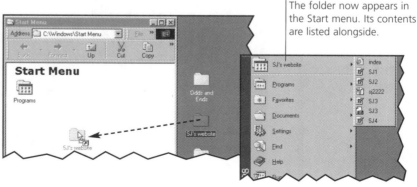

EMBEDDED DOCUMENTS

That method is fine if you happen to have the document, folder or program in a handy position on the Desktop. Sometimes, however, you might find that it's embedded in a chain of sub-folders. Rather than "digging" it out, you can use an alternative method to place it in the Start menu. Begin by right-clicking on a neutral area of the Taskbar.

1 Select <u>PROPERTIES</u> from menu. In the <u>TASKBAR</u> <u>PROPERTIES</u> dialog box, click on the <u>START</u> <u>MENU PROGRAMS</u> tab. Click on <u>ADD</u>.

2 In the <u>CREATE</u> <u>SHORTCUT</u> dialog box, click on <u>BROWSE</u> and select the document. Click on <u>OPEN</u> and then on <u>NEXT</u>.

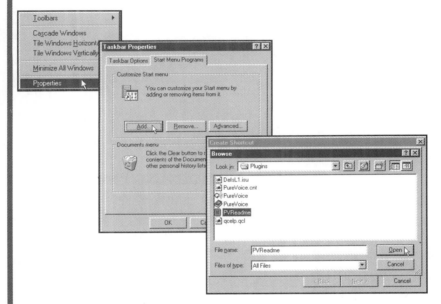

3 Select the folder in which the document should appear in the Start menu. Finally, type a name to identify your new shortcut.and click on <u>FINISH</u>.

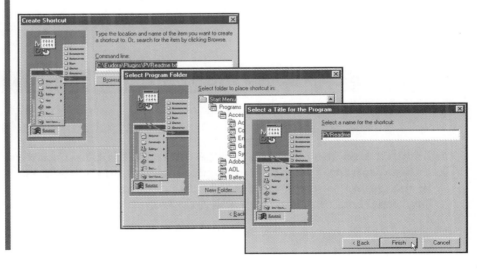

REMOVING FROM THE START MENU

Taking an entry out of the Start menu is a good deal easier than adding one. All you have to do is drag it out and drop it wherever you like. In this example we'll remove the entry we set up on the previous page and dump it in the Recycle Bin.

1 Click on the <u>START BUTTON</u>, select the entry you want to remove and hold the mouse button. Drag and drop the icon into the <u>RECYCLE BIN</u>.

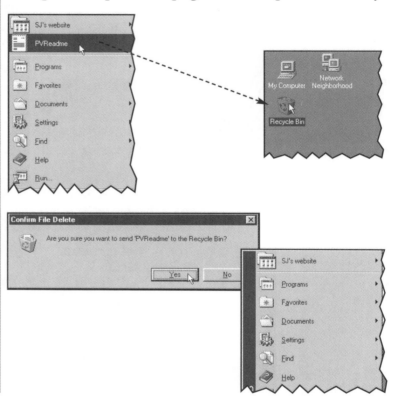

2 You are asked to confirm that you want this entry to go into the Recycle Bin. Click on <u>YES</u>. If you click on the <u>START BUTTON</u> you can see in the Start Menu that the entry is no longer there.

AUTOMATIC STARTUP

If you regularly have the same programs running when you use your PC, a really smart move is to have Windows 98 start them up for you each time you switch on. Here is how you do it in four easy steps:

1. Right-click on the <u>START BUTTON</u>. From the pop-up menu choose <u>OPEN</u>.
2. In the <u>Open Start Menu</u> window, double-click on <u>PROGRAMS</u>.
3. In the <u>Open Programs</u> window, double-click on <u>STARTUP</u>.
4. Any programs that you drag and drop from the Desktop will be stored as shortcuts.

Next time you start Windows 98, these programs will be automatically launched.

PERSONAL MATTERS

6

If there's one word that truly sums up Windows 98, it's "versatile". Not only are there numerous ways of perfoming the same tasks, but you can also alter numerous settings to meet your own requirements or tastes. If you want the screen to look different, you can change it; if you want the mouse to respond in a different way, you can make it do so. Many other possibilities for personalizing your PC are shown in this chapter.

THE CONTROL PANEL

All the settings you need to access for personalizing your PC are neatly grouped together in one window called the CONTROL PANEL. From re-configuring your modem to altering the screen resolution – it all starts here.

VIEWING THE CONTROL PANEL

The two most obvious ways of getting to the Control Panel are from the Windows 98 menu, or from My Computer.

1 Click on the START button. Choose SETTINGS from the WINDOWS 98 pop-up menu. Click on CONTROL PANEL.

OR

Double-click on MY COMPUTER. When the folder opens, double-click on CONTROL PANEL.

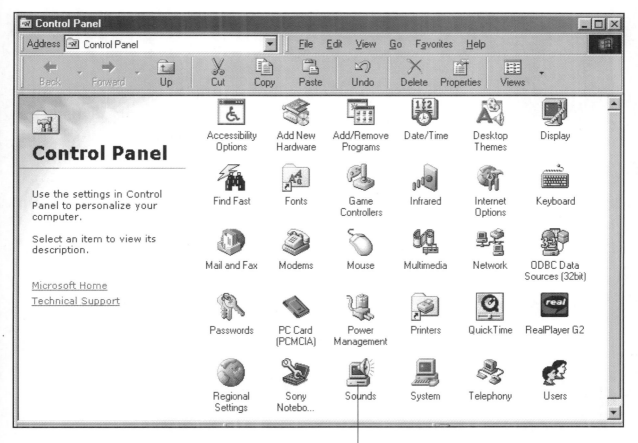

Double-click on icons to launch each function.

CONTROL PANEL CONTENTS

If you compare the contents of your own Control Panel with the one shown above, you'll probably find that they are not exactly the same. This is quite normal; the contents will simply depend on the type of PC you have. Furthermore, as you install additional hardware or software, icons that control some of their settings will usually appear in the Control Panels Window. Over the coming pages we'll take a detailed look at how you can use some of the Control Panel functions to personalize your PC. Right at the end of the chapter you'll find a brief description of some of the icons and some tips on how you can use them.

DATES AND TIMES

It may seem obvious, but setting the correct date and time on your computer is a basic necessity. This is not only necessary to allow your PC to act as a clock, but is also required by your software's basic calendar functions. Also, every time you create or edit a file, the date and time you worked on it is stored on your hard disk. This gives you a record of exactly when you made these changes.

VIEWING THE DATE AND TIME WINDOW

By opening the Date/Time window not only can you change your PC's calendar settings but also the time zone in which you are working. As with all of the functions in this chapter, begin with an open Control Panel window.

1 Double-click on the DATE/TIME icon. The DATE/TIME PROPERTIES window appears. Click on the DATE & TIME tab.

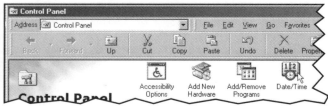

To select the month, click on the arrow and choose a name from the drop-down menu.

To select the day, click on any of the numbers.

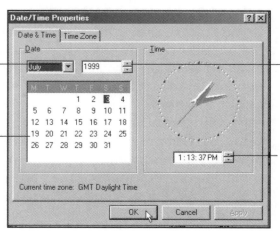

Select the year by clicking on the up or down spin buttons.

Set the current time by highlighting a part of the time (for example the hour) and clicking on the up or down spin buttons. Alternatively, you can type it in using the format hh:mm:ss AM/PM.

CHANGING THE TIME ZONE

The global traveller can also alter the PC's time zone from within the Date/Time Properties window.

1 Click on the TIME ZONE tab. Click on the arrow to select a new time zone.

2 Select a new time zone from the drop-down menu. Click on APPLY and then OK.

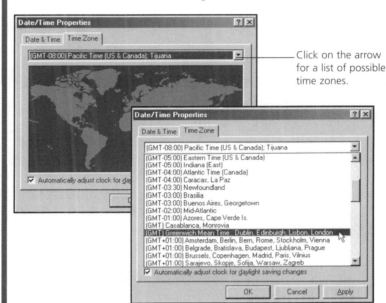

Click on the arrow for a list of possible time zones.

DISPLAYING THE TIME IN THE TASKBAR

You can set up your PC so that the current time is always displayed on the screen.

1 Right-click on an empty space in the task bar. From the pop-up menu, click on PROPERTIES. In the TASKBAR PROPERTIES dialog box, click on the TASKBAR OPTIONS tab. Tick the SHOW CLOCK box. Click OK.

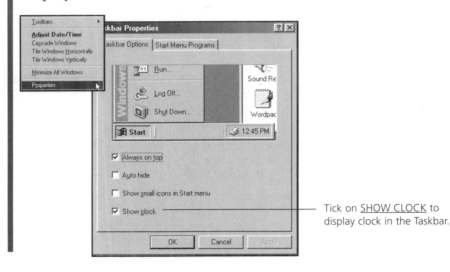

Tick on SHOW CLOCK to display clock in the Taskbar.

CHANGING THE DESKTOP

If you click on the Display icon in the Control Panel you can change the way in which various aspects of your Desktop appear.

DISPLAY PROPERTIES

When you click on Display, the Display Properties dialog box appears. Among other things, this allows you to alter the background appearance of your Desktop, change the way text appears within a window, and set up a screen saver.

1 Click on the DISPLAY icon. The DISPLAY PROPERTIES dialog box.

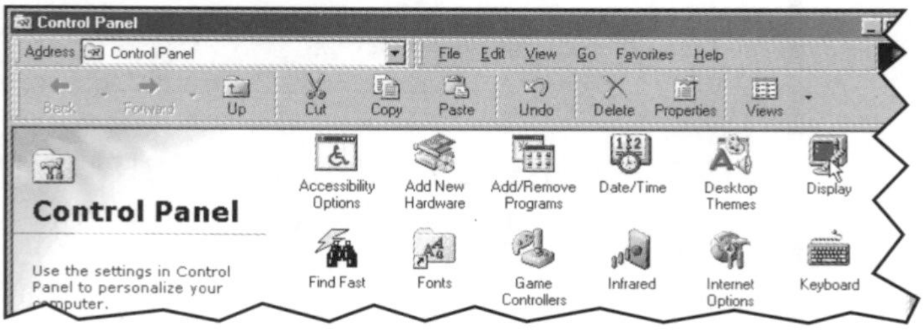

2 Click on the BACKGROUND tab. Use the WALLPAPER selection area to choose an image for display on your desktop

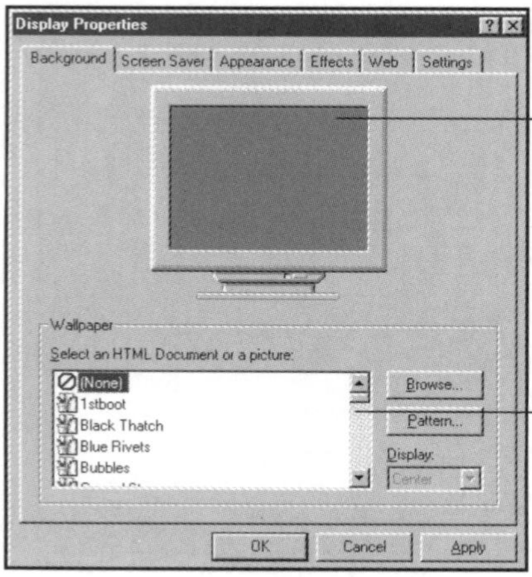

The current wallpaper is displayed here.

Select your wallpaper from the list and click on APPLY to see it displayed in the screen above.

3 New wallpaper is displayed in the screen and on the desktop. Click <u>OK</u> when you are happy with your selection.

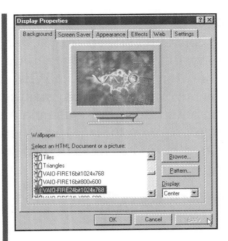

APPEARANCE OPTIONS

You can use the Appearance options to change the way in which the windows themselves appear.

1 Click on the <u>APPEARANCE</u> tab in the <u>DISPLAY PROPERTIES</u> dialog box.

2 Select a new appearance from the <u>SCHEME</u> box. Click on <u>APPLY</u>.

3 You can see the effect of your change in the top half of the screen. If you want to store it click on <u>OK</u>, otherwise on <u>CANCEL</u>.

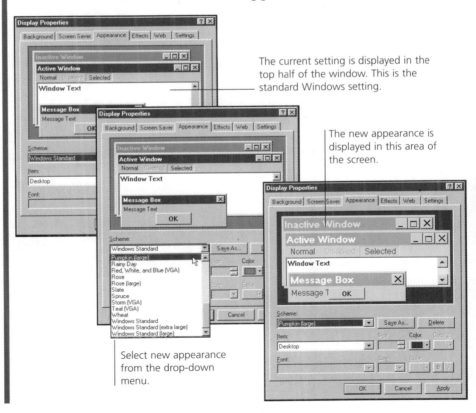

The current setting is displayed in the top half of the window. This is the standard Windows setting.

The new appearance is displayed in this area of the screen.

Select new appearance from the drop-down menu.

SCREEN SAVERS

Heavily used computer screens can suffer from a problem known as "burn-in". This occurs when the same image is left on the screen for too long a period. When this happens, your screen loses some of its sharpness, making it less pleasant to view. You can avoid burn-in by using a screen saver. This is a little animation program that cuts in when a PC has been idle for a pre-defined period of time. Screen savers are not only useful but can also be highly entertaining.

1 Open the DISPLAY PROPERTIES dialog box and click on the SCREEN SAVER tab. Click on the arrow alongside the SCREEN SAVER box and choose your selection from the drop-down menu.

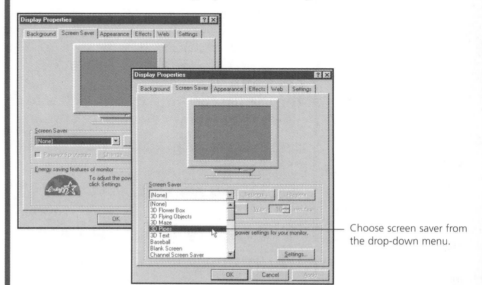

Choose screen saver from the drop-down menu.

2 The screen saver is shown in miniature in the top half of the window. To see a full-size example, click on the PREVIEW button.

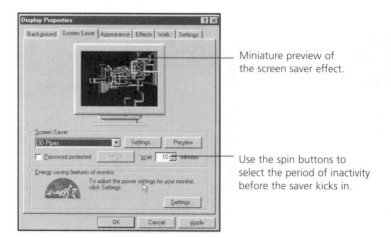

Miniature preview of the screen saver effect.

Use the spin buttons to select the period of inactivity before the saver kicks in.

3 To see if there are any further configuration choices for this screen saver, click on SETTINGS in the SCREEN SAVER area.

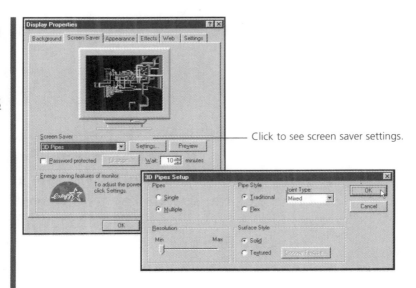

Click to see screen saver settings.

PASSWORD CONTROL

You can use a screen saver as an additional security control. If you don't want anyone looking at your PC when you are not at your desk, you can set up the screen saver so that a password has to be entered in order to get back to the Desktop. Be careful, though; if you forget the password you could end up getting locked out of your own PC!

1 Click on the PASSWORD PROTECTED box. To set the password click on CHANGE. Enter the details in the CHANGE PASSWORD dialog box. Click on OK.

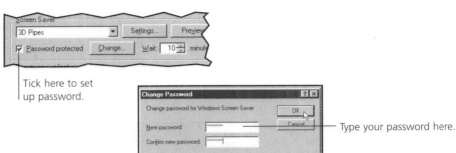

Tick here to set up password.

Type your password here.

ENERGY SAVINGS

If you click on SETTINGS in the ENERGY FEATURES OF MONITOR area, you will see the Windows 98 POWER MANAGEMENT window. This gives you a number of energy saving options, such as resting the monitor and hard disk. Like screen savers, these features can be programmed to take effect after a specific time. You can see how the POWER MANAGEMENT features work on pages 118-119.

KEYBOARD AND MOUSE

The Control Panel's Keyboard and Mouse options allow you to change the way in which they perform in Windows 98; for example, the rate at which the cursor blinks, or the speed at which double-clicks of the mouse launch a program or open a folder. This may not seem like much, but if you use your PC a lot you will soon discover the benefits of tailoring the way it works to your needs.

KEYBOARD
To alter the keyboard configuration, double-click on the Keyboard icon in the Control Panels window.

1 Click on the KEYBOARD icon in the CONTROL PANEL. The KEYBOARD PROPERTIES dialog box appears.

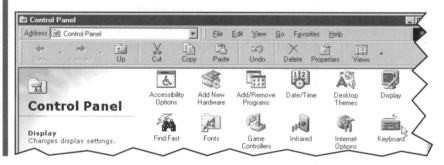

KEYBOARD VERSUS MOUSE

Sometimes Windows 98 can be so flexible that it almost hurts. Many first-timers are bamboozled by the fact that there seem to be dozens of alternative ways to perform the same simple tasks. Using the mouse is the most straightforward way of manouvering around your desktop, but when you're working at high speed it can sometimes be difficult for the mouse to keep up with you. Luckily Windows 98 provides you with a selection of handy keyboard shortcuts, many of which use the ALT key. By combining the ALT key with other keys you can invoke selections from the drop-down menu without even laying a finger on the mouse. A full list of these shortcuts can be found on pages 170-173.

2 To alter the various speed parameters, select the <u>SPEED</u> tab at the top of the box. When you have made your choices click on <u>OK</u>.

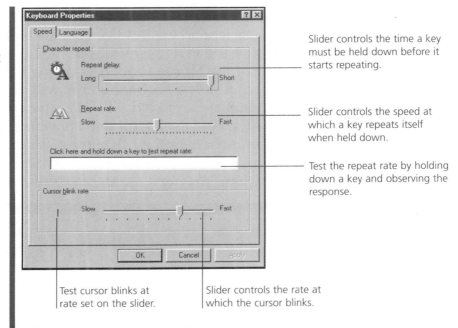

Slider controls the time a key must be held down before it starts repeating.

Slider controls the speed at which a key repeats itself when held down.

Test the repeat rate by holding down a key and observing the response.

Test cursor blinks at rate set on the slider.

Slider controls the rate at which the cursor blinks.

3 If you want to change your PC's language and alphabet attributes, click on the <u>LANGUAGE</u> tab.

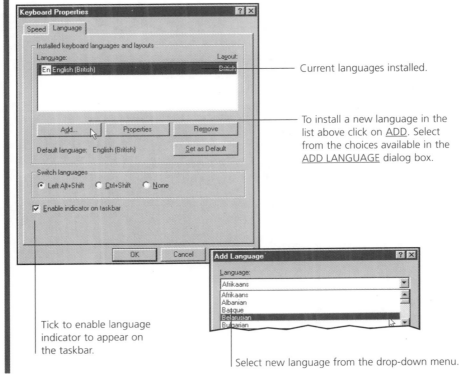

Current languages installed.

To install a new language in the list above click on <u>ADD</u>. Select from the choices available in the <u>ADD LANGUAGE</u> dialog box.

Tick to enable language indicator to appear on the taskbar.

Select new language from the drop-down menu.

MOUSE MATTERS

The Mouse icon in the Control Panel is there so that you can personalize the various settings for your mouse. The precise contents of the Mouse Properties dialog box, which appears when you double-click on the icon, will depend on the type of mouse you have installed. This example uses a "VersaPad" mouse – the kind used with some notebook PCs – which has a greater number of options than most others. All of the examples shown here will be possible with all types of mouse – although you may have to search through the different tabs to find them.

1 Double-click on the <u>MOUSE</u> icon in the <u>CONTROL PANEL.</u> The <u>MOUSE PROPERTIES</u> dialog box appears.

2 Click on the <u>BUTTONS</u> tab. This allows you to switch roles for the two mouse buttons. (This makes life easier for left-handed PC users.)

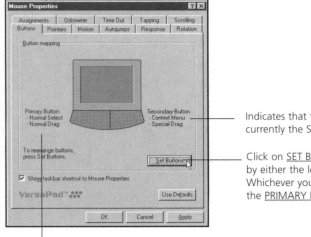

Indicates that the right button is currently the SECONDARY BUTTON.

Click on <u>SET BUTTON</u> followed by either the left or right button. Whichever you choose becomes the <u>PRIMARY BUTTON</u>.

Indicates that the left button is currently the PRIMARY BUTTON.

3 Click on the RESPONSE tab. This page has options for you to alter the speed at which the mouse responds to a double-click. On some MOUSE PROPERTIES dialog boxes this information appears on the BUTTONS page.

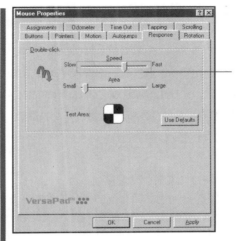

Move the slider to the left to slow down the response of the mouse; move it to the right to speed it up.

4 Click on the MOTION tab to alter the sensitivity of mouse movement.

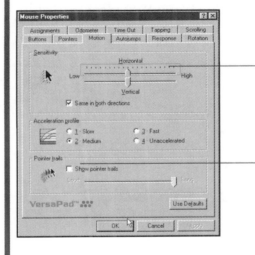

Move the upper slider to control horizontal response; move the lower slider to control vertical response.

Tick here to show the motion trail of the mouse arrow.

4 Click on the POINTERS tab to alter the way in which the mouse cursor appears on screen.

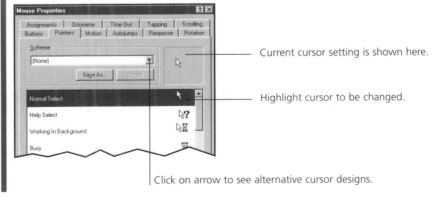

Current cursor setting is shown here.

Highlight cursor to be changed.

Click on arrow to see alternative cursor designs.

SOUND EFFECTS

If you have a soundcard fitted, you can't fail to have noticed the assortment of noises that emerge from your PC at various choice moments. If you take a look at the Sounds option in the Control Panel you can see how they are programmed.

SOUNDS AND SCHEMES

Sounds within your PC may be tied up to specific events. For example, every time you maximize a screen your PC can be programmed to play a set sound. You can either program individual sounds to accompany events or you can choose a "scheme" – which is an entire set of sounds linked to different possible sets of events.

1 Double-click on the <u>SOUNDS</u> icon in the <u>CONTROL PANEL.</u> The <u>SOUNDS PROPERTIES</u> dialog box appears.

2 To link a sound to an event, select an event from the <u>EVENTS</u> menu. Choose the sound that will accompany that event from the <u>NAME</u> list. Click on <u>OK</u>. In this example, a sound called "Robotz Maximize" will play each time you <u>MAXIMIZE</u> a window.

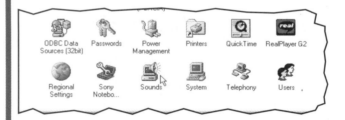

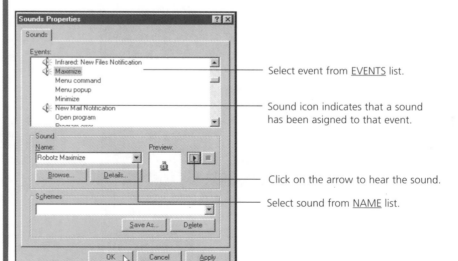

Select event from <u>EVENTS</u> list.

Sound icon indicates that a sound has been asigned to that event.

Click on the arrow to hear the sound.

Select sound from <u>NAME</u> list.

2 To select a set of sounds, choose from the options in the SCHEMES drop-down list. Click on APPLY.

3 You will be asked if you want to save your old settings as a scheme. If you want to, click on YES. Type a name to identify your sound scheme in the SAVE SCHEME AS dialog box and click on OK.

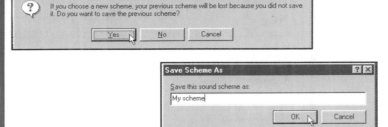

ADDING YOUR OWN SOUNDS

You can add your own sounds to the Control Panel using Windows 98's Sound Recorder, which is a very basic digital audio recorder. You need an input source, such as a microphone, or the output from a CD player, then all you do is click on the record button. Sound Recorder creates what are known as "Wav" files (so-called because they are suffixed with ".wav" To make your sounds accessible to the Control Panel they must be copied into the MEDIA folder, which is in the WINDOWS folder on your hard disk. Take care when recording sounds – they really eat into your memory. It's no coincidence that most of Windows 98's pre-recorded sounds are barely a second in length.

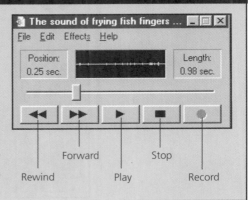

SUMMARY OF ICONS

Here is brief run-down of the most commonly found Control Panel icons.

ACCESSIBILITY OPTIONS
A variety of screen, keyboard and mouse options that make Windows 98 easier to use for people with disabilities.

ADD NEW HARDWARE
Windows 98 "Plug and Play" system uses the ADD NEW HARDWARE WIZARD to make installing new hardware more straightforward.

ADD/REMOVE PROGRAMS
Click to install a new piece of software onto your PC or remove existing software from your hard disk.

DATE/TIME
Click on this icon to reset your system date and time. You can also use it specify your global time zone.

DESKTOP THEMES
Instead of setting up your wallpaper, appearances, screen savers and sounds individually, you can adopt a theme which sets them up as a group.

DISPLAY
Use this setting to change wallpaper, screen savers, colours, screen resolution, size and colour of windows, text and many other parameters.

FONTS

This icon is actually a shortcut to the Fonts folder in which you install new fonts. Double-click on the icon to see which fonts are loaded on your PC.

GAME CONTROLLERS

Used to configure different joysticks. Windows 98 generally uses "Plug and Play" for automatic installation of such hardware.

INFRARED

Monitors "wireless" infrared communication between notebooks or some other peripheral devices, such as suitably equipped printers.

INTERNET OPTIONS

Can be used to set up and monitor most of the basic Internet configurations. Many of these can also be set up from Internet Explorer.

KEYBOARD

Alters the various keyboard attributes such as speed of repeated keys, language formats or keyboard types.

MODEMS

Tells you the kind of modem, if any, that you have installed. Also allows you to complement or adjust current settings.

MOUSE

Alters the various parameters relating to your mouse. Options will vary depending on the sophistication of your mouse.

MULTIMEDIA

Property settings for audio, video, MIDI and audio CD. Most commonly used to control recording output and recording levels.

PASSWORDS
Different personalized settings can be created for PCs with more than one regular user. Settings can be controlled by password.

PC CARD (PCMCIA)
Credit-card-sized circuit that plugs into a slot in the side of a notebook PC. Contains modem or interfaces with other external hardware components.

POWER MANAGEMENT
Controls energy conservation on notebook PCs. Can also be configured to turn off monitors and hard disks after periods of inactivity.

PRINTER
Shortcut icon to the Printer set up program. This configures all the information necessary to run printers or fax cards.

REGIONAL SETTINGS
Configures changes in the basic settings for numbers, currencies, date and time in different parts of the world.

SOUNDS
Links different sounds to different events. Can either be programmed on an individual basis or entire sets (schedules) can be configured.

SYSTEM
Double-click on System to tweak hardware profiles, view details of peripheral devices and performance statistics.

USERS
Double-click to activate "multi-user profiles". Useful if your PC is used by more than one person as it allows personal settings to be stored.

THE FREEBIES

Although a fine piece
of software in its own right,
as we've already seen,
Windows 98 isn't really that
much use unless you are
intending to run other
programs. As with previous
versions of Windows, Microsoft
have thoughtfully provided
some pretty basic, but useful
programs as a part of the
package. This chapter will show
you how to use some of them.

7

W**HERE ARE THEY?**

You can find the "free" programs that come with
Windows 98 by pressing the <u>START</u> button and
choosing <u>PROGRAMS</u> from the flip-up menu. They
are all located in the <u>ACCESSORIES</u> folder.

1 Click on <u>START</u>
and then choose
<u>PROGRAMS</u> from
the flip-up menu.

2 From the menu
list that appears
alongside
<u>PROGRAMS</u> choose
<u>ACCESSORIES</u>.

3 From the menu
list that drops
down alongside
<u>ACCESSORIES</u> select
the program or folder
you wish to access.

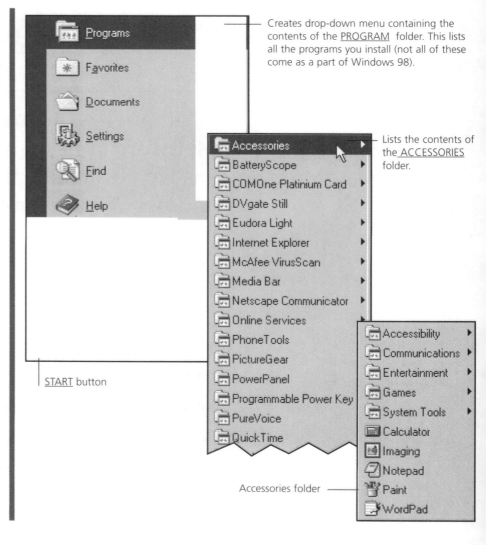

Creates drop-down menu containing the
contents of the <u>PROGRAM</u> folder. This lists
all the programs you install (not all of these
come as a part of Windows 98).

Lists the contents of
the <u>ACCESSORIES</u>
folder.

<u>START</u> button

Accessories folder

CALCULATOR

You may be surprised how quickly you come to rely on your Windows 98 calculator. You can enter details by clicking on the buttons of the on-screen keypad, or by typing them directly from your keyboard.

1 To open the program, select <u>CALCULATOR</u> in the <u>ACCESSORIES</u> menu.

2 The "standard" CALCULATOR window opens. To open the more advanced calculator, select <u>SCIENTIFIC</u> in the <u>VIEW</u> menu.

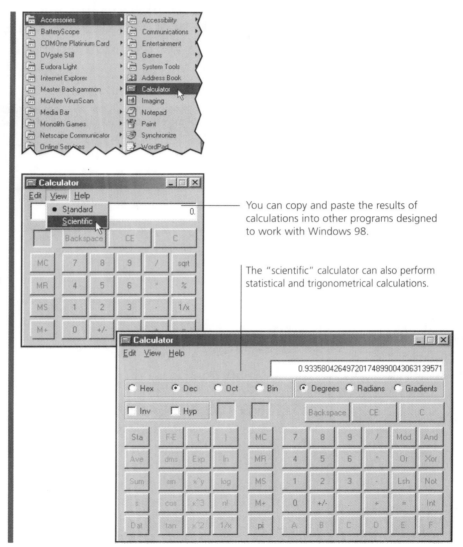

You can copy and paste the results of calculations into other programs designed to work with Windows 98.

The "scientific" calculator can also perform statistical and trigonometrical calculations.

WORDPAD

One of the programs you'll find in the Accessories folder is called WordPad. This is a very simple word processor, which works rather like a typewriter on which you can change text once it's been written. You might have heard of another Microsoft program called Word. Whilst WordPad is nothing like as sophisticated as Word, it can still do almost all of the things most of us want from a word processor.

1 To open WordPad, double-click on <u>WORDPAD</u> in the <u>ACCESSORIES</u> menu.

2 WordPad opens a new document called <u>UNTITLED</u>. The cursor positions itself at the top of the screen. To enter text you simply start typing.

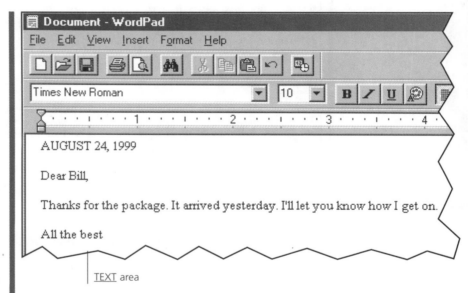

<u>TEXT</u> area

ALTERING THE APPEARANCE OF TEXT

WordPad comes with its own Windows-style menu bar that allows you to alter the way in which your document looks after you've typed it. You can, for example, alter the appearance of the text by changing its size or font. You can make it appear in bold, italic or underlined style. Do this by positioning the cursor at the start of the text you want to change, clicking on the mouse and dragging it to the end of the text you want to change. When you release your finger from the mouse button the text will be highlighted and ready for you to change. This example shows you how to change the size of the text and the font. You can read more about fonts on page 170.

1 With the text highlighted, position the mouse on the arrow alongside the FONT SIZE menu. Click and hold, dragging the mouse over the menu options. Release the button when you reach the required option.

2 The text (which has now been changed from 10pt to 20pt), remains highlighted. To alter the font, position the mouse above the arrow on the FONT STYLE menu, dragging the mouse over the menu options. Release the button when you reach the required option. In this example, a font called VERDANA (CENTRAL EUROPEAN) was chosen.

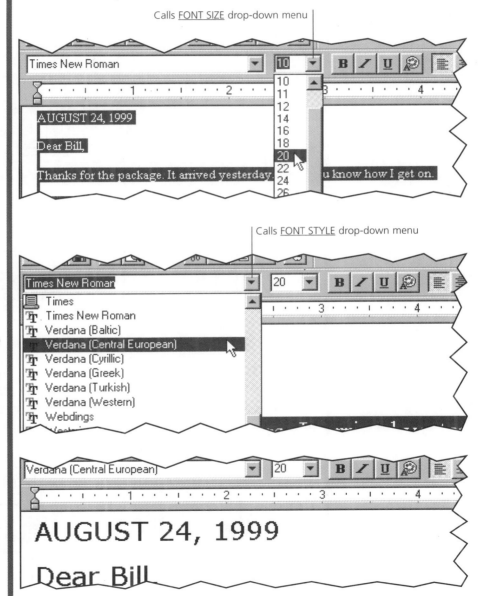

Calls FONT SIZE drop-down menu

Calls FONT STYLE drop-down menu

WORDPAD TOOLBAR

The toolbar at the top of the window provides shortcuts to some of the more common functions. You can also perform all of these tasks by choosing options from the drop-down menus, but the toolbar provides speedier access. For example, you can create a new blank WordPad document by clicking on the "Open new document" button (on the top left of the toolbar) or by choosing <u>NEW</u> from the <u>FILE</u> menu.

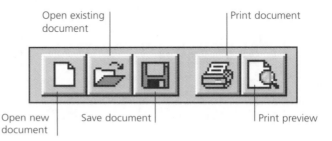

Open existing document | Print document

Open new document | Save document | Print preview

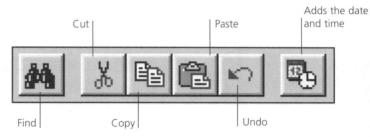

Cut | Paste | Adds the date and time

Find | Copy | Undo

TEXT TOOLBAR

You've already seen how the font and size can be changed from the text toolbar. You can also alter the styling and colour of the text, as well as its "ranging" (i.e. the vertical margin to which it aligns).

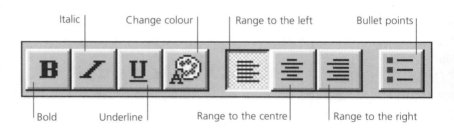

Italic | Change colour | Range to the left | Bullet points

Bold | Underline | Range to the centre | Range to the right

NON RECHARGEABLE BATTERIES ARE NOT TO BE RECHARGED.
DO NOT USE RECHARGEABLE BATTERIES
RETAIN PACKAGING FOR REFERENCE.
DIFFERENT TYPES OF BATTERIES OR NEW AND USED BATTERIES ARE NOT TO BE MIXED.
ONLY BATTERIES OF THE SAME OR EQUIVALENT TYPE AS RECOMMENDED ARE TO BE USED.
BATTERIES ARE TO BE INSERTED WITH THE CORRECT POLARITY.
EXHAUSTED BATTERIES ARE TO BE REMOVED FROM THE TOY.
THE SUPPLY TERMINALS ARE NOT TO BE SHORT-CIRCUITED.

LES PILES NON RECHARGEABLES NE DOIVENT PAS ETRE RECHARGEES.
NE PAS UTILISER DE PILES RECHARGEABLÊS.
CONSERVER L'EMBALLAGE : RÉFÉRENCES FABRICANT.
NE PAS MELANGER DES PILES DE TYPES DIFFERENTS OU DES PILES NEUVES ET USAGEES.
N'UTILISER QUE LES PILES DE MEME TYPE QUE CELUI CONSEILLE OU DE TYPE EQUIVALENT.
LES PILES DOIVENT ETRE INSTALLEES AVEC LA BONNE POLARITE.
LES PILES USEES DOIVENT ETRE ENLEVES DU JOUET.
NE PAS COURCURCUITER LES BORNES DES PILES.

IKKE GENOPLADELIGE BATTERIER MA IKKE GENOPLADES.
GEBRUIK GEEN HERLAADBARE BATTERIJEN.
OPBEY EMBALLAGE FOR REFERENCE.
FORSKELLIGE TYPER BATTERIER ELLER GAMLE & NYE BATTERIER MA ALDRIG BLANDES.
KUN BATTERIER AF SAMME ELLER LIGNENDE TYPE SOM ANBEFALES MA BENYTTES.
BATTERIER SKAL ILAEGGES KORREKT (POLARISERING +/-).
OPBRUGTE BATTERIER BOR FJERNES FRA LEGETØJET.
BATTERIKONTAKTERNE MA IKKE KORTSLUTTES.

DE NIET-OPLAADBARE BATTERIJEN NIET HEROPLADEN.
ALKALINE-BATTERIJEN TESAMEN GEBRUIKEN.
VERPACKKING BEWAREN VOOR REFERENTLE.
GEEN VERSCHILLENDE SOORTEN OF NIEUWE EN OUDE BATTERIJEN MENGEN.
GEBRUIK ENKEL AANBEVOLEN BATTERIJEN OF EQUIVALENTEN.
DE BATTERIJEN MOETEN MET DE JUISTE POLARITEIT GEINSTALLEER WORDEN.
GEBRUIKTE BATTERIJEN UIT HET SPEELGOED HALEN.
DE KLEMMEN VAN DE BATTERIJEN NIET KORTSLUITEN.

NICHT RECYCELBARE BATTERIEN KONNEN NICHT ENTSORGT WERDEN BZW. WERDEN NICHT ZURUCKGENOMMEN.
KEINE RECYCELBARE BATTERIEN VERWENDEN.
VERPACKUNG AUFBEWAHREN, ENTHÄLT HERSTELLERANGABE.

ZUSAMMEN MIT ...

NUR BATTERIEN DES GLEICHEN ODER EQUIVALENTEN TYPES WIE EMPFOHLEN VERWENDEN.
BATTERIEN NUR MIT DEN KORREKTEN POLARISIERUNG EINSETZEN.
VERBRAUCHTE BATTERIEN SIND DEM SPIELZEUG ZU ENTNEHMEN.
DIE VERKAUFSSTANDE MÜSSEN DIE VERMEIDUNG EINES KURZSCHLUSSES GEWÄHRLEISTEN.

LADDA ALDRIG ETT ICKE ÅTERUPPLADDNINGSBART BATTERI.
ANVÄND EJ UPPLADDNINGSBARA BATTERIER.
BEVARA FÖRPACKNINGEN SOM REFERENS.
BLANDA ALDRIG OLIKA ELLER GAMLA OCH NYA BATTERIER.
ENBART BATTERIER AV SAMMA SORT BÖR ANVÄNDAS.
SÄTT I BATTERIERNA MED POLERNA P RÄTT HÅLL.
TA ALLTID UR FÖRBRUKADE BATTERIER UR LEKSAKEN.

AS PILHAS NAO DEVEM SER RECARREGÁVEIS, NAO DEVEM SER RECARREGADAS.
NÃO USAR PILHAS RECARREGÁVEIS.
CONSERVE A EMBALAGEM. REFERÊNCIAS DO FABRICANTE.
NAO MISTURAR PILHAS NOVAS COM USADAS, NEM MISTURAR PILHAS DE TIPOS DIFERENTES.
NAO UTILIZAR OUTRAS PILHAS QUE NAO SEJAM AS RECOMENDADAS OU EQUIVALENTES.
AS PILHAS DEVEM SER COLOCADAS NA POLARIDADE CORRECTA.
AS PILHAS USADAS DEVEM SER RETIRADAS DO BRINQUEDO.
NAO SE DEVE FAZER CURTO CIRCUITO COM OS TERMINAIS DAS PILHAS.

NON RICARICARE MAI LE BATTERIE NON RICARICABILI.
NON USARE PILE RICARICABILI.
CONSERVARE L'IMBALLO REFERENZE FABBRICANTE.
NON MESCOLARE BATTERIE DI TIPO DIFFERENTE O PILE NUOVE ED USATE.
UTILIZZARE SOLO IL TIPO DI BATTERIE RACCOMANDATO O UN TIPO EQUIVALENTE.
LE BATTERIE VANNO INSERITE CON LA POLARITA GIUSTA.
LE BATTERIE SCARICHE DEVONO ESSERE RIMOSSE DAL GIOCATTOLO.
EVITARE DI TOCCARE I CONTATTI.

LAS PILAS NO RECARGABLES NO DEBEN SER RECARGADAS.
NO UTILIZAR PILAS RECARDABLES.
CONSERVAR EMBALAJE CON SEÑAS FABRICANTE.
NO MEZCLAR PILAS DE DIFERENTES TIPOS NI NUEVAS CON USADAS.
NO UTILIZAR OTRAS PILAS QUE NO SEAN LAS RECOMENDADAS O EQUIVALENTES.
LAS PILAS DEBEN SER POSICIONADAS CON LA POLARIDAD CORRECTA.
LAS PILAS USADAS DEBEN RETIRARSE DEL JUGUETE.
LOS TERMINALES DE LAS PILAS NO DEBEN SER CORTO-CIRCUITADOS.

CHARACTER MAP

Character Map allows you to look at each individual character in any font that is loaded on your PC. It also allows you to copy any character into the document on which you are currently working.

1 To open the program, choose the CHARACTER MAP option from the SYSTEM TOOLS menu.

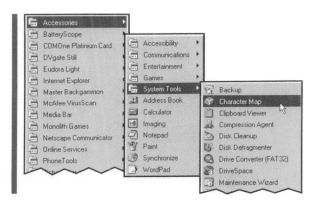

Accessories ▶
BatteryScope
COMOne Platinium Card
DVgate Still
Eudora Light
Internet Explorer
Master Backgammon
McAfee VirusScan
Media Bar
Monolith Games
Netscape Communicator
Online Services
PhoneTools

Accessibility ▶
Communications ▶
Entertainment ▶
Games ▶
System Tools ▶
Address Book
Calculator
Imaging
Notepad
Paint
Synchronize
WordPad

Backup
Character Map
Clipboard Viewer
Compression Agent
Disk Cleanup
Disk Defragmenter
Drive Converter (FAT32)
DriveSpace
Maintenance Wizard

Click to COPY the contents of the CHARACTERS TO COPY box onto the Clipboard so that it can be pasted into any document.

Click and hold down the mouse to magnify the character.

Select font

Character Map

Font: 𝕋 AvantGarde Bk BT ▾   Characters to copy: [   ]   Close

Select

Copy

Shows available characters in the selected font.   Keystroke: Q

Click on SELECT to position character in the CHARACTERS TO COPY box.

PAINT

Another excellent Windows 98 freebie is Paint; a very simple drawing program which allows you to create your own designs or modify scanned images. You can simulate drawing with a pencil, paintbrush or even an airbrush. You can also add text to your pictures.

1 Click on <u>PAINT</u> in the <u>ACCES-SORIES</u> menu.

2 To begin your drawing, choose the tool you want to use – such as the paintbrush – from the <u>TOOLBOX</u>. Click and drag the mouse in the drawing area to create your image.

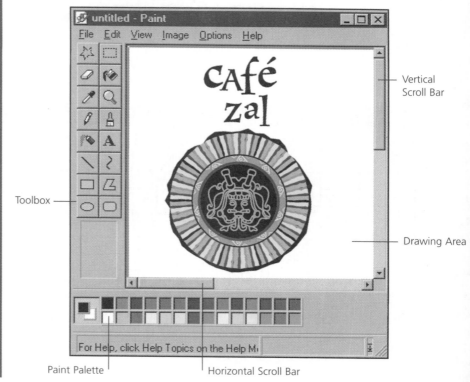

Toolbox

Vertical Scroll Bar

Drawing Area

Paint Palette

Horizontal Scroll Bar

DIPPING INTO THE TOOLBOX

Paint comes alive when you select one of the tools and begin dragging the mouse across the screen of your PC. The Paint Toolbox contains features that not only help you to create images but also allows you to alter them afterwards. For example, you can change their shape, colour, or even erase them. Each of the tools are described below.

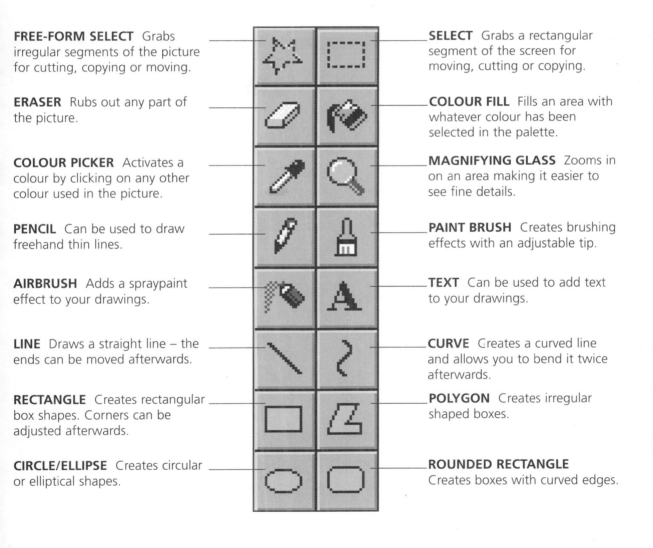

FREE-FORM SELECT Grabs irregular segments of the picture for cutting, copying or moving.

SELECT Grabs a rectangular segment of the screen for moving, cutting or copying.

ERASER Rubs out any part of the picture.

COLOUR FILL Fills an area with whatever colour has been selected in the palette.

COLOUR PICKER Activates a colour by clicking on any other colour used in the picture.

MAGNIFYING GLASS Zooms in on an area making it easier to see fine details.

PENCIL Can be used to draw freehand thin lines.

PAINT BRUSH Creates brushing effects with an adjustable tip.

AIRBRUSH Adds a spraypaint effect to your drawings.

TEXT Can be used to add text to your drawings.

LINE Draws a straight line – the ends can be moved afterwards.

CURVE Creates a curved line and allows you to bend it twice afterwards.

RECTANGLE Creates rectangular box shapes. Corners can be adjusted afterwards.

POLYGON Creates irregular shaped boxes.

CIRCLE/ELLIPSE Creates circular or elliptical shapes.

ROUNDED RECTANGLE Creates boxes with curved edges.

PHONE DIALER

If you have a modem fitted to your computer you can use Windows 98's speed dial facility – Phone Dialer. All you do is click on the speed dial buttons and your PC will ring the number for you.

1 From the ACCESSORIES menu select COMMUNICATIONS and select PHONE DIALER from the drop-down menu.

2 The PHONE DIALER window appears.

Number can also be entered directly from the keyboard.

Click on any named button to speed-dial pre-defined numbers.

Click to call the number shown in the NUMBER TO DIAL box.

You can enter a telephone number by clicking on the number buttons.

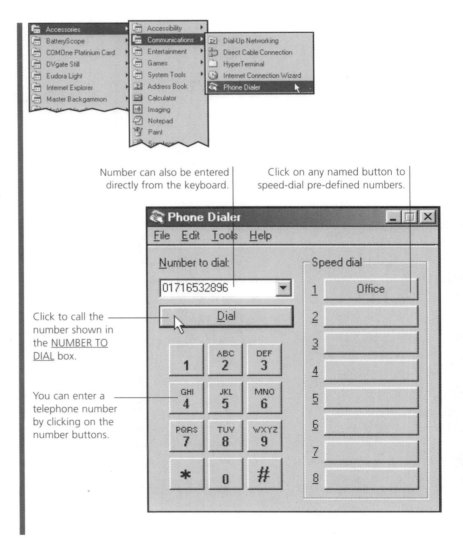

3 To set up a new speed-dial, click on an empty button. The PROGRAM SPEED DIAL window appears.

4 Enter the name you want to appear on the button and the telephone number. Click on SAVE.

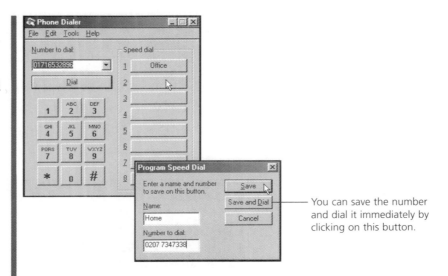

You can save the number and dial it immediately by clicking on this button.

DIALING PROPERTIES

To configure settings relating to the outgoing telephone call, you can use the Dialing Properties feature.

1 In the PHONE DIALER window, select DIALING PROPERTIES from the TOOLS menu.

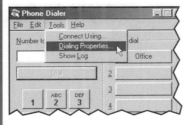

2 Specify the relevant details in the DIALING PROPERTIES dialog box.

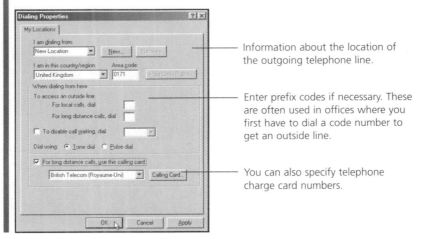

Information about the location of the outgoing telephone line.

Enter prefix codes if necessary. These are often used in offices where you first have to dial a code number to get an outside line.

You can also specify telephone charge card numbers.

CD PLAYER

As long as your PC is fitted with a soundcard, speakers and a CD-ROM drive, you can listen to CDs using Windows 98's handy CD Player program.

1 From the ACCESSORIES menu select ENTERTAINMENT. Then select CD PLAYER from the drop-down menu. The CD window appears.

Track number — [05] 00:05

Transport controls

Artist: New Artist <G:>

Title: New Title

Track: Track 5 <05>

Total length of CD — Total Play: 73:01 m:s

Track: 02:56 m:s — Length of current track

2 To change the volume, double-click on the loudspeaker icon in the Windows Taskbar.

If you click and hold on the icon a single pop-up volume control will appear.

3 The VOLUME CONTROL window appears.

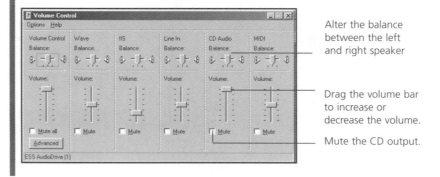

Alter the balance between the left and right speaker

Drag the volume bar to increase or decrease the volume.

Mute the CD output.

IMAGING FOR WINDOWS

Kodak's Imaging For Windows allows you to alter scanned pictures. Whilst it's not quite a full photo-editing suite, you can still neatly integrate images and text, and it can also come in handy for converting different types of file format.

1 From the ACCESSORIES menu select IMAGING.

2 You can select a document by choosing OPEN in the FILE menu.

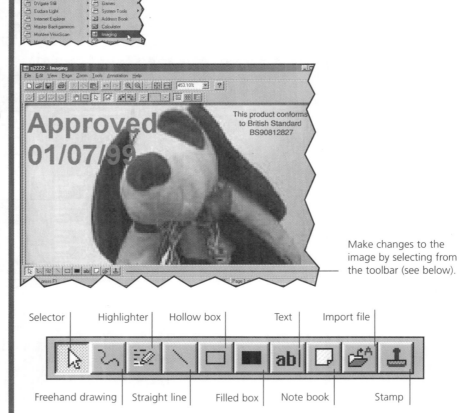

Make changes to the image by selecting from the toolbar (see below).

Selector | Highlighter | Hollow box | Text | Import file

Freehand drawing | Straight line | Filled box | Note book | Stamp

GAMES

OK, Windows 98 isn't exactly giving you the latest blockbuster game as a free gift, but you do get four little distractions with which you can pass the time. They also make good mouse practice for beginners!

1 From the ACCESSORIES menu select GAMES. The folder contains four options: FREECELL; HEARTS; MINESWEEPER; and SOLITAIRE.

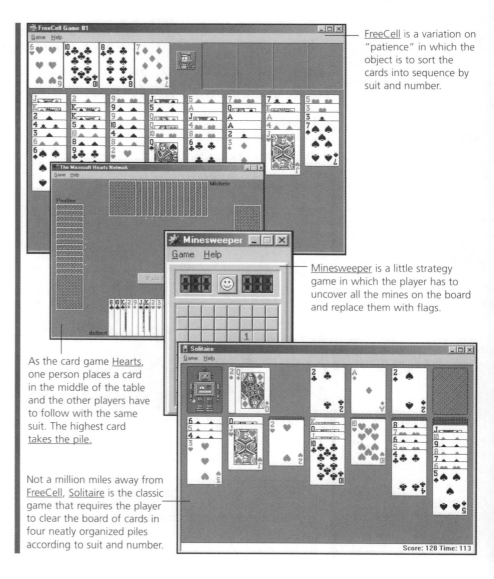

FreeCell is a variation on "patience" in which the object is to sort the cards into sequence by suit and number.

Minesweeper is a little strategy game in which the player has to uncover all the mines on the board and replace them with flags.

As the card game Hearts, one person places a card in the middle of the table and the other players have to follow with the same suit. The highest card takes the pile.

Not a million miles away from FreeCell, Solitaire is the classic game that requires the player to clear the board of cards in four neatly organized piles according to suit and number.

TUNING YOUR SYSTEM

Windows 98 automatically installs a series of programs to make your system more efficient and reliable. Although software like ScanDisk and FAT 32 Drive Converter may not be up there with the classics in the entertainment stakes, they really are useful to know about. Not only can they make your PC run faster but they can also perform vital repair jobs on your hard disk.

||NTRODUCING THE SYSTEM TOOLS

If you own a car, it's a matter of common sense that if you perform periodic maintenance (like topping up the oil or keeping the tyres at the correct pressure) it will drive better and your car will last longer. PCs are not that different. It's a good idea to get into the habit of making regular checks on the state of your hard disk. Windows 98 provides some useful programs to help you keep your PC performing at its best.

WHERE ARE THE TOOLS?

You will find the Windows 98 <u>SYSTEM TOOLS</u> folder grouped together in the <u>ACCESSORIES</u> folder.

1 Click on the <u>START</u> button. From the menu select <u>PROGRAMS</u>. From the <u>PROGRAMS</u> folder select <u>ACCESSORIES</u>. From the <u>ACCESSORIES</u> folder select <u>SYSTEM TOOLS</u>. This folder contains all of the system utilities that come as a part of Windows 98.

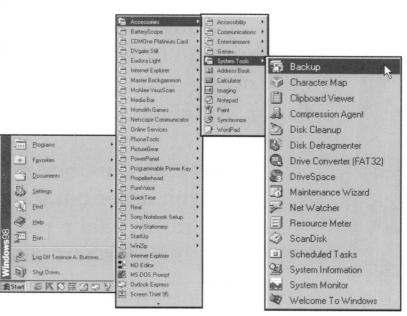

DISK PROPERTIES
A good place to start your routine maintenance is to look at your hard disk's PROPERTIES dialog box. This will provide you with some clues as to its current state of health.

1 Double-click on MY COMPUTER to open up the folder. Right-click on your hard disk drive and select PROPERTIES from the drop-down menu.

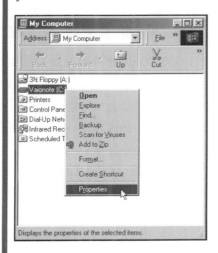

2 The PROPERTIES dialog box appears. Click on the GENERAL tab to see the current status of the disk. Click on the TOOLS to run the system utilities.

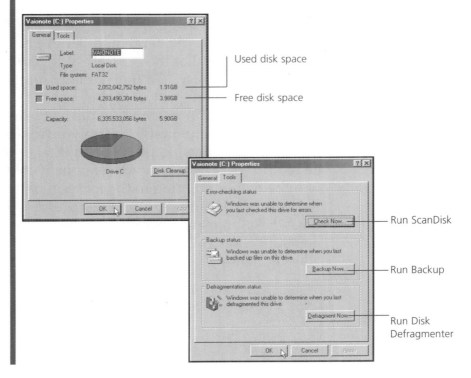

Used disk space

Free disk space

Run ScanDisk

Run Backup

Run Disk Defragmenter

D ISK DEFRAGMENTER

You can view a computer's hard disk as a massive matrix in which every piece of information is broken down into its smallest component (a binary digit) and placed in its own exclusive slot. For a file (which is a group of data) to be accessed as quickly as possible, the binary digits should be held together in a single block. This is not always possible, so different parts of the same file are held on different parts of the disk. When this happens it is called "fragmentation".

WHY IS IT A PROBLEM?

Imagine trying to fit a large number of groupings of people into a cinema so that they can all sit together. When the cinema is empty this is easy, but it eventually reaches a point where the groups have to split up if they are to find a seat. Files on hard disks work in much the same way – if disk space gets low, then fragmentation is the only possibility. The problem is that if files become too fragmented it takes longer for them to be read. This is because every fragment contains an extra piece of information pointing to the location of the next fragment in the chain. It doesn't damage your files or your hard disk, but it does make your processor work unneccesarily hard, and will generally slow things down. You can sort out this problem by "defragmenting" your hard disk periodically.

1 Click on DISK DEFRAGMENTER in the SYSTEM TOOLS menu.

2 Select the drive you wish to defragment and click on <u>OK</u>.

Before you click on <u>OK</u>, remember that "defragging" a hard disk can take several hours, depending on its size and how fragmented the files are.

3 The status box marks out the progress.

4 If you click on SHOW DETAILS you can see the defragmentation in progress.

Click on LEGEND for the colour-coded key to each piece of data.

5 At the end of defragmentation a completion box will appear. Click on <u>YES</u> to quit.

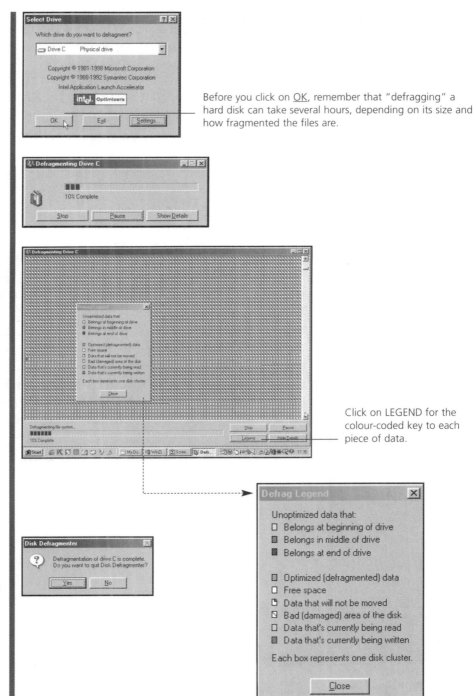

SCANDISK

Sometimes a PC loses track of where a piece of data is stored on the hard disk. This can happen when parts of a file are written to a "bad sector". ScanDisk not only analyses these problems but can usually repair them as well.

WHAT DOES IT DO?

ScanDisk looks for common hard disk errors such as "lost" file fragments which it reports back to you and informs you about any it finds in a report at the end of the scan. If you tick the box marked <u>AUTOMATICALLY FIX ERRORS</u> it will try to repair these fragments without first informing you. If it fails to find the related files it can delete these fragments. The program also identifies cross-linked files, where two different pointers are looking at the same piece of data.

ScanDisk uses two modes of operation: in <u>STANDARD</u> mode, it checks the files and folders for errors; in <u>THOROUGH</u> mode, it reads and writes back each cluster of data on the hard disk. Whereas <u>STANDARD</u> mode takes a few minutes to run, <u>THOROUGH</u> mode will take considerably longer, depending on the size of the hard disk. A sensible way to use ScanDisk is to run it first in "quick" mode and then if disk errors still occur try the more time-consuming alternative. More advanced users of Disk Defragmenter will want to take advantage of some of ScanDisk's advanced features.

1 Click on <u>SCANDISK</u> in the <u>SYSTEMS TOOLS</u> folder.

2 Click on the drive on which you want to run ScanDisk. Then click the ADVANCED button.

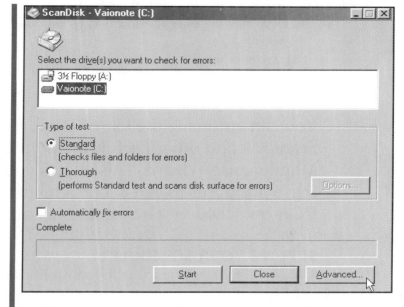

3 Specify the required options and click OK.

Many of these options determine what ScanDisk does with lost file fragments after it has located them.

MAINTENANCE WIZARD

You can automate the use of Disk Defragmenter, ScanDisk and other useful functions by using the Maintenance Wizard. This allows you to schedule these programs to run at convenient times when your PC is switched on but you are not actually using it.

SETTING YOUR SCHEDULE?

The Maintenance Wizard is the most efficient way to keep your hard disk in trim. It ensures that your programs run faster, the system is "tuned" for optimum performance and that free disk space is maximized. Maintenance Wizard is essentially a "macro" program. This means that it does nothing of its own accord other than sequence instructions to run other programs. Disk Defragmenter is run first, followed by ScanDisk, and then Windows 98 is instructed to delete temporary files.

Don't forget that although you can set Maintenance Wizard so that it runs in the middle of the night, your PC still has to be switched on for it to work.

1 Click on MAINTENANCE WIZARD in the SYSTEMS TOOLS folder. In the dialog box that appears, select the EXPRESS option. Click on NEXT.

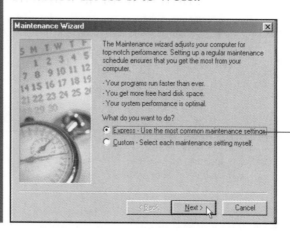

EXPRESS uses the most common settings for ScanDisk and Disk Defragmenter; CUSTOM allows you to enter your own settings.

HOW OFTEN?

Routine hard disk maintenance can be a tedious business. It can take hours to "defrag" a large hard disk, and while that's going on you can't use your PC. That's why Maintenance Wizard is such a handy system tool – you can leave it to do its business overnight. How often you need to perform these functions will largely depend on what you do with your PC. Once a month will be enough for most domestic users, but if you are working with large files, such as those used in audio recording or video editing, you may need to do it every few days if you are to guarantee optimal performance.

2 Select the range of times for your maintenance schedule and click on NEXT.

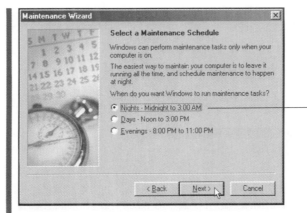

Choose one of the options to select the times at which Maintenance Wizard will run.

3 The final window gives a summary of the tasks that will be performed and the time they will take place. Click on FINISH to activate the schedule.

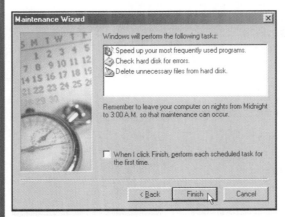

4 To change your schedule, re-run the program and click on the CHANGE button. Click on OK.

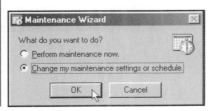

DISK CLEANUP

Like many offices and desks, it's easy for your PC to get clogged up with junk. Windows 98 gives you a neat solution called Disk Cleanup, a program that can be used to delete temporary files, downloaded Internet programs and the contents of the Recycle Bin.

1 Choose <u>SYSTEM TOOLS</u> in the <u>ACCESSORIES</u> menu and then click on <u>DISK CLEANUP</u>.

2 Select the drive you want to clean from the <u>SELECT DRIVE</u> window and then click on <u>OK</u>.

3 Make your selection from the FILES TO DELETE window. Click on <u>OK</u>.

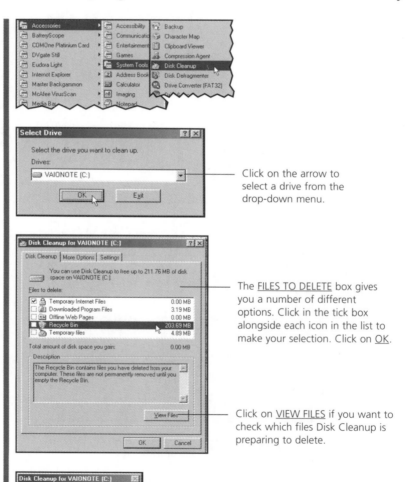

Click on the arrow to select a drive from the drop-down menu.

The <u>FILES TO DELETE</u> box gives you a number of different options. Click in the tick box alongside each icon in the list to make your selection. Click on <u>OK</u>.

Click on <u>VIEW FILES</u> if you want to check which files Disk Cleanup is preparing to delete.

3 If you want to delete the files click on <u>YES</u>.

DRIVE CONVERTER (FAT 32)

One way of making more space available on your hard disk is to convert your drive to FAT 32 format using the Drive Converter (FAT 32) program. This also improves the time it takes your programs to launch.

1 Choose <u>SYSTEM TOOLS</u> in the <u>ACCESSORIES</u> menu and then click on <u>DRIVE CONVERTER (FAT 32)</u>.

2 Click on <u>NEXT</u> in the <u>DRIVE CONVERTER (FAT 32)</u> dialog box. In the next dialog box, choose the hard disk you want to convert. Click on <u>NEXT</u>. The conversion will begin.

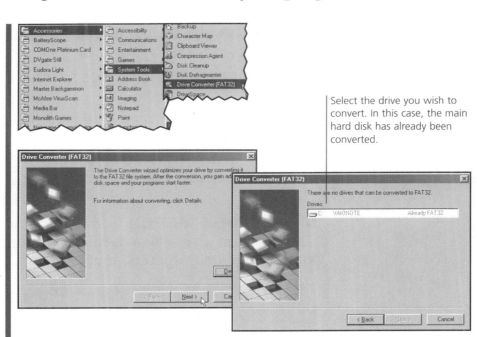

Select the drive you wish to convert. In this case, the main hard disk has already been converted.

FAT 32 CONSIDERATIONS

Whilst the benefits are great, there are a few things you might want to bear in mind before deciding to convert from the original Windows FAT (File Allocation Table) system to FAT 32. To begin with, your drive must be more than 512 MB in volume. Also, once you've converted, you can't revert to the original system, or uninstall Windows 98 in favour of an earlier version. FAT 32 also means that you can't use the free DriveSpace 3 utility, which compresses the data on your hard disk, almost doubling your capacity.

SYSTEM STUFF

In the SYSTEMS TOOLS folders you'll come across several seemingly inscrutable options which you may want to investigate if you are of a technical inclination.

SYSTEM MONITOR

If you run system monitor in the background it will provide a graphical representation of your PC's processing performance. To launch the program choose <u>SYSTEM TOOLS</u> in the <u>ACCESSORIES</u> menu and then click on <u>SYSTEM MONITOR</u>.

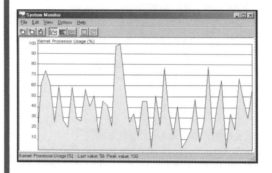

SYSTEM INFORMATION

This program gives you a detailed run-down of the way nearly every imaginable aspect of your PC is configured.

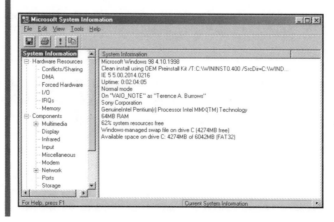

SYSTEM INFORMATION TOOLS MENU

As well as all the pages of configuration data, System Information also has some useful active functions in its own right. These can be found in the Tools menu.

1 Click on the TOOLS menu in the MICROSOFT SYSTEM INFORMATION window.

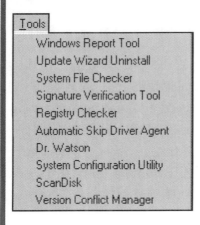

SYSTEM FILE CHECKER

Choose the SYSTEM FILE CHECKER to verify your system files and reinstate those that have been corrupted.

1 In the TOOLS menu, select SYSTEM FILE CHECKER.

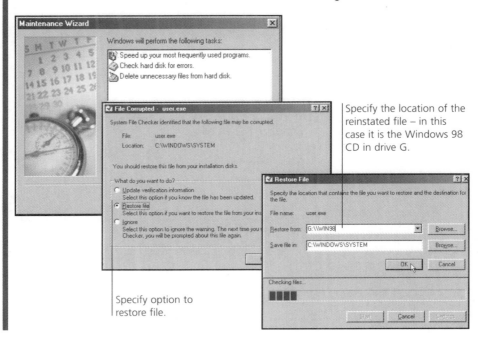

Specify the location of the reinstated file – in this case it is the Windows 98 CD in drive G.

Specify option to restore file.

POWER MANAGEMENT

Not strictly a SYSTEM TOOL in the same sense as the others in this chapter, the POWER MANAGEMENT feature allows you to save energy by turning off the monitor and hard disk when not in use. This saves power and boosts the life of the components. It can make a major difference to notebook PCs using re-chargeable batteries.

POWER MANAGEMENT FUNCTIONS

To locate the program, click on START, SETTINGS and CONTROL PANEL.

1 Double-click on the POWER MANAGEMENT icon. The POWER MANAGEMENT PROPERTIES dialog box appears.

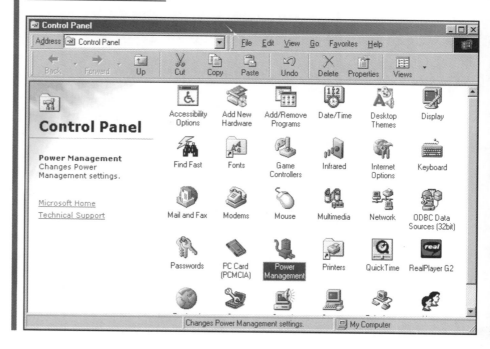

2 To select a ready made setting, click on the arrow alongside the POWER SCHEMES box, choose an option from the list, and then click on OK. To select the intervals after which the monitor and hard disk are switched off, use the bottom two boxes in the same way.

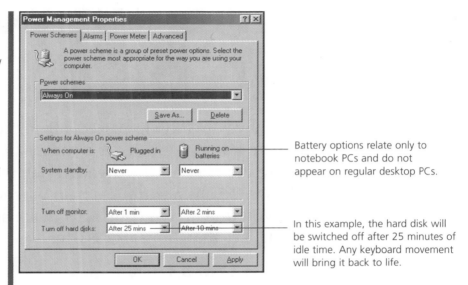

Battery options relate only to notebook PCs and do not appear on regular desktop PCs.

In this example, the hard disk will be switched off after 25 minutes of idle time. Any keyboard movement will bring it back to life.

POWER ALARM

Since power is such a crucial issue for notebook PCs, the POWER MANAGEMENT PROPERTIES dialog box contains additional features with such models in mind. For example, you can set the controls so that they give off an alarm when the battery is close to running out.

2 Click on the ALARMS tab. Set the points at which the power alarm will set off. Click on ALARM ACTION to set the alarm details.

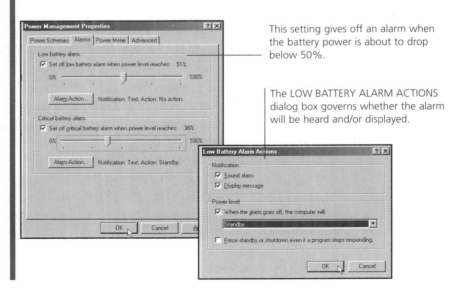

This setting gives off an alarm when the battery power is about to drop below 50%.

The LOW BATTERY ALARM ACTIONS dialog box governs whether the alarm will be heard and/or displayed.

BACKING UP YOUR HARD DISK

As we have already discussed, all storage media have a finite lifespan. In practice this means that you have to prepare yourself for the dreaded day when your hard disk dies. This is a complete pain whenever it happens, but if you don't have your hard disk backed up it's nothing less than a major disaster.

WHEN YOUR HARD DISK EXPIRES

Unless you've had a lucky break, if your hard disk packs in then there's a good chance that you are going to lose all of the data held onboard. If it's something extremely valuable you can take your old drive to a "disk doctor", who'll physically dismantle it and try to salvage something from the mess. He'll also charge you a hefty fee for trying. If you make regular backups, at least when disaster strikes you can shrug your shoulders, fit a new hard disk drive, restore your files and generally feel rather pleased with yourself.

WHAT IS BACKING UP, AND HOW DO YOU DO IT?

The term "backup" simply refers to copies of files from your hard disk stored somewhere else. You can backup onto other hard disks, recordable CD-ROMs, Zip or Jaz cartridges, or (if you're feeling masochistic) dozens and dozens of floppy disks.

It's easy enough to make copies of working files periodically, but the problem with this ad hoc approach is in its lack of organization. One of Windows 98's system tools – Backup – provides you with a framework for systematically carrying out this vitally important function. When you run Backup, the BACKUP WIZARD is launched. Like other Windows 98 wizards, this takes you step-by-step through the whole process, helping you create a BACKUP JOB. The program lets you decide which files need to be backed up, where you want them to be backed up and whether or not you want your backed up data to be compressed. Once you have set up the basic "job" – which can be time-consuming – the settings are stored so that in future you can repeat the process with little more than a few clicks of your mouse.

1 Select <u>SYSTEM TOOLS</u> in the <u>ACCESSORIES</u> menu, and then click on <u>BACKUP</u>.

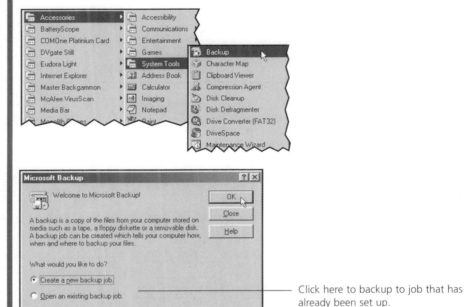

2 The <u>MICROSOFT BACKUP</u> dialog box appears. Click on <u>CREATE A NEW BACKUP JOB</u>, and then on <u>OK</u>.

Click here to backup to job that has already been set up.

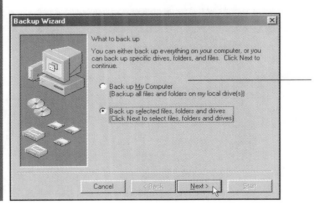

3 The <u>BACKUP WIZARD</u> dialog box is launched. Click on the <u>BACKUP SELECTED FILES</u> option and then <u>NEXT</u>.

Clicking on the first option backs up ALL files and folders on the hard disk.

4 Select the files that you want to back up. Folders appear in the left-hand column – click on the folder to see its contents shown in the right-hand box. To select a file, click on the tick box alongside its icon.

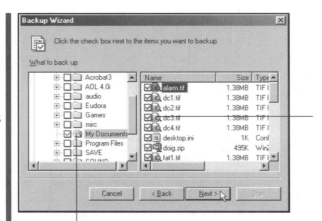

Tick alongside the icon indicates that the file is to be backed up.

Faded tick indicates that not all files within that folder are for backup.

5 To backup all of the files chosen in the previous dialog box, click on <u>ALL SELECTED FILES</u> and then on <u>NEXT</u>.

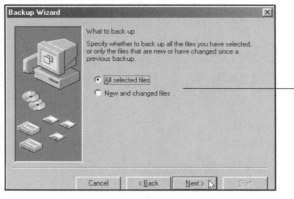

Select this option to only backup new and altered files.

6 Select the location to which the backed up file will be written. Click on <u>NEXT</u>.

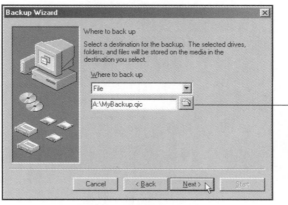

Click here to choose location where more than one possibility exists. In this example (since the files are relatively small) floppy disks are being used to backup.

7 Click on the two tick boxes to have the integrity of the backup verified, and the backed up file compressed. Click on NEXT.

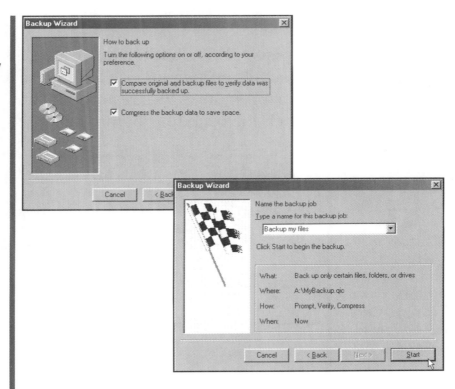

8 Enter the name of your backup file and then check that the options you have selected are all correct. Click on START.

9 The BACKUP PROGRESS window tells you the time remaining until the backup is complete. On completion, click on OK. To close down Backup, press ALT+4.

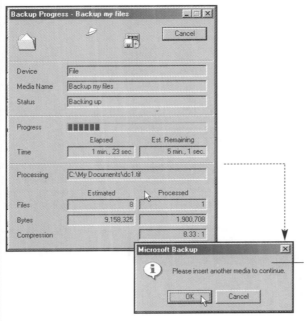

You will get this message if your media device runs out of space. In this case, a second floppy disk is required.

RESTORES

The reverse of a backup, a "restore" is quite simply the act of retrieving a backed up file (or set of files). To use Windows 98's restore function, you have to launch the backup program again.

1 Click on the RESTORE tab. Click on the RESTORE FROM arrow. The RESTORE FROM dialog box appears. Select your restore archive and click on OPEN. Back on the main page, select the files you want to restore. Click on START.

Select files to be restored in the same way as those backed up on page 168.

2 The program will prompt you to ensure that the external media device is ready to transfer the files. Click on OK.

3 The RESTORE PROGRESS window appears. Click on OK when it has finished.

Message indicates status of job – if anything goes wrong, an error message will appear.

Meter bar indicates how much of the job has been done.

E-MAIL AND THE INTERNET

The Internet is THE buzz word of the moment. And the good news is that with the INTERNET EXPLORER and OUTLOOK EXPRESS programs installed as standard features, WINDOWS 98 is arguably the best platfrom from which to launch into cyberspace. This chapter gives you a basic guide to getting connected, sending e-mails and surfing the World Wide Web.

WHAT IS THE INTERNET?

If you link two or more computers together it creates what is known as a "network". The Internet is the greatest network of them all, linking millions of computers all over the world so that their owners can communicate and exchange information.

WHAT CAN YOU DO WITH IT?

The Internet is all about communication. Not only can you make contact with other Internet users on a one-to-one or group basis, but you can also access an incredibly wide range of information which is held on "servers" across the world. Indeed, the Internet could be viewed as the greatest repository of information ever to have been assembled. Here is a brief run-down of some of the most common Internet pursuits.

E-MAIL

Instead of taking your letters to the post office, buying stamps and then putting them in the postbox, you can type a message into your computer, connect to the Internet and press a button. It should arrive at its destination anywhere in the world within a few minutes for the cost of a quick local telephone call.

THE WORLD WIDE WEB

The Web is like one big multimedia program. Using INTERNET EXPLORER, which comes with WNDOWS 98, you can read pages of text, listen to music, look at images and watch video clips. Web sites may be advertisements for products, art galleries, reference libraries, online stores where you can buy products with your credit card, fan sites devoted to bands, sports or hobbies, or even simply a few pages about the author.

Web sites are also fairly easy to set up for yourself, so if you have a particular hobby or interest you can share it with other like-minded users all over the world.

GROUP ACTIVITIES

A newsgroup is rather like a public notice board on which messages can be posted, read and responded to. There are many thousands of different newsgroups on the Internet many of which cover VERY specific subjects.

A downside of e-mail or newsgroups is that conversations can only take place in "real" time if everyone is permanently online - which would be an expensive business. One way in which real-time communication is possible is by using an online chat system such as Internet Relay Chat. IRC software connects groups of people in "virtual" rooms. Each time you type a message at the bottom of the screen the other people in the room will immediately see the message and can respond.

DON'T YOU HAVE TO BE A GEEK?

Some would have you believe that the Internet is the realm of the sad and lonely nerd. Nothing could be further from the truth. The Internet has something for EVERYONE irrespective of age, sex or interests. It really is the greatest communications revolution since the advent of television.

HOW DID THE INTERNET COME ABOUT?

Although widely viewed as a 1990s phenomenon, the Internet first came to life in 1969 when the US Department of Defense commissioned a massive military computer network called ARPANET. The idea was that if a base was disabled by a nuclear strike the network of computers would not be broken – the remaining bases would still be able to communicate with one another online. The system involved breaking information down into small "packets" of data which were then sent around the network before being reassembled at their destination. If one of the computers in the network failed to work, the packets would simply find alternative routes. When the US military abandoned ARPANET in 1982, the remains became known as the Internet, which was quickly taken up by colleges and other scientific foundations in the US. In the late 1980s, commercial organizations linked to the Internet began to sell their own connections to the public. These companies, usually called ISPs (Internet Service Providers) are connected to the Internet via high-speed routing links. Whenever we think of ourselves as being connected to the Internet, we are actually linked to our ISP's computer system which passes and receives messages to and from the rest of the Internet for us.

INTERNET BASICS

Getting connected to the Internet is a straightforward business. All you need is a PC, a modem, a standard telephone line and an account with a service provider who will give you access to the Internet. Most of the software you need comes as a part of Windows 98.

MODEMS

Your computer connects to a regular domestic telephone line through a piece of hardware called a modem. This links you directly to your service provider – the supplier that gives you access to the Internet. A modem converts digital signals into a format that can be passed along a telephone line.

Modems are now extremely cheap to buy, although if you've acquired a new computer over the past year or so, there's a good chance that it already has one fitted. A modem will either be a physical box that connects between your computer and the telephone or a piece of electronic circuitry that slots neatly inside the computer's casing. Both types work equally well.

The most important technical feature to worry about is the speed at which a modem can transmit and read data. This is measured in "bits per second". The fastest standard modem that most Internet service providers can deal with is 56K (56,000 bits per second) – it's not worth bothering with anything slower. This speed is sometimes referred to as "V.90".

Other features to look out for are fax and voice support. Some modems allow you the handy facility for transmitting and receiving faxes on your computer – some can also double-up as telephone answering machines.

WHAT'S A SERVICE PROVIDER?

Companies selling or giving Internet access can be categorized as Internet Service Providers (ISPs) or Online Service Providers (OSPs). The vast majority of Internet companies fall into the first category. An ISP simply gives you a means of connecting to the Internet. This will include a unique e-mail address as well as space for you to create your own Web pages. Online Service Providers (OSPs) also give these features but present the Internet to you through their own easy-to-use entry menus (see the example at the foot of the page). The advantage of using these access providers – the biggest of which is AOL – is that it makes using all areas of the Internet simple for beginners. Furthermore, the OSPs each have specialized services which are only accessible to their subscribers. The downside is that the amount of money you pay each month usually depends on the length of time you have been connected to the Internet, so for heavy users it can be an expensive business.

Some ISPs simply charge a signing-on fee and a fixed monthly charge irrespective of online time, although a rapidly growing development has been the birth of "free" ISPs. These companies make their money through advertising or through deals with telecommunications companies – the only charges to the consumer are for technical support.

As always, different people have different needs, so before you subscribe to any of these services you should understand exactly what you'll be getting for money.

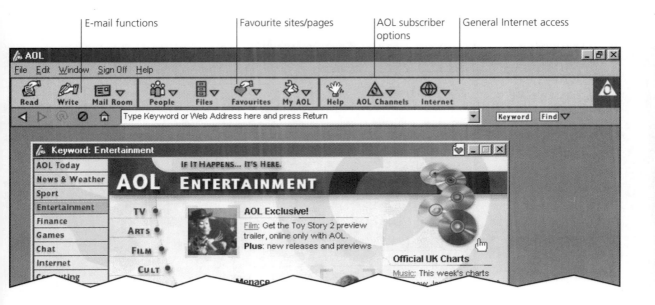

LOGGING ON

To show you how easy it can be to set up an Internet account, we'll create one using FreeServe, which is Britain's biggest ISP. Connection is free. All you need to get started is the CD, which is widely available in high-street stores.

1 Click on the FreeServe icon in the CD drive. In the welcome screen. Click on INSTALL FREESERVE.

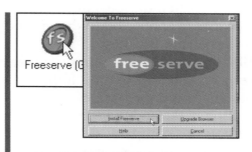

2 The process begins with the installation of Internet Explorer. Follow the steps, each time clicking on NEXT until installation is complete. Clicking on FINISH will cause the computer to restart.

3 On restart, FreeServe's set-up screen starts automatically. Click on CONTINUE to start up the INTERNET CONNECTION WIZARD. This connects you to the Internet.

Your computer "calls" the number which was just installed with Internet Explorer.

4 If the connection was successful you will see the ONLINE SIGNUP SCREEN. To get to the next stage, click on REGISTER FOR A NEW ACCOUNT. Before you get to your account details you are asked to fill in some personal details about yourself and your interests.

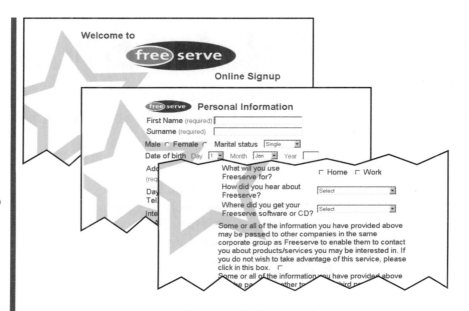

5 Specify your e-mail address and password. Make a note of this information – you will need it in future.

Choose an e-mail address for yourself here. As long as no other customer of that ISP uses the same address, it will be accepted.

6 If your e-mail address and password are both valid click on FINISHED. You now have an Internet account.

E-MAIL BASICS

In spite of the increasing popularity of the World Wide Web, e-mail still accounts for the vast majority of online usage.

HOW DOES E-MAIL WORK?

E-mail is an extremely simple concept. You run a program that lets you type a letter, then you enter an e-mail address, connect to the Internet and press a button to send it. The same software can also be used to read e-mails that have been sent to you. What happens, though, if the person to whom you are writing is not online when you send the message? Unlike sending a fax to someone whose machine is turned off - an e-mail message just sits there waiting for you. The message is held on the mail server of your ISP. Each time you run your e-mail software it sends a note to the mail server to find out if you have any new mail. If there is some, then the message is downloaded onto your computer. It's as simple as that.

USING OUTLOOK EXPRESS

You don't need to buy new software to read or write e-mails because Outlook Express has already been installed as a part of Windows 98 with Internet Explorer.

Before your e-mail software will work you have to configure it so that can send and retrieve mail from your ISP's mail servers. To do this there are a few simple pieces of information you need to know: your e-mail address, the name of your ISP's outgoing mail server (usually the SMTP server), the name of the incoming mail server (usually a POP3 server) and the user ID and password you need to access the POP3 server. You should be given this information when you set up your account, but if not, a quick telephone call to your ISP should solve the problem. When you run the program for the first time you should be prompted to enter this information by the INTERNET CONNECTION WIZARD.

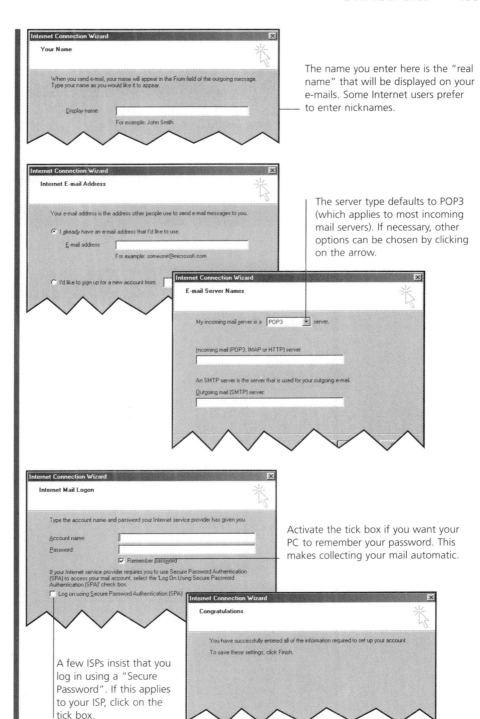

1 Enter your name and click on NEXT.

The name you enter here is the "real name" that will be displayed on your e-mails. Some Internet users prefer to enter nicknames.

2 Enter the e-mail address given to you by your ISP. Click on NEXT.

The server type defaults to POP3 (which applies to most incoming mail servers). If necessary, other options can be chosen by clicking on the arrow.

3 Enter the names of the incoming and outgoing mail servers. Click on NEXT.

4 Enter your POP 3 user ID and password. Click on NEXT.

Activate the tick box if you want your PC to remember your password. This makes collecting your mail automatic.

5 Click on FINISH. You are now ready to send and receive e-mails.

A few ISPs insist that you log in using a "Secure Password". If this applies to your ISP, click on the tick box.

WRITING AN E-MAIL

When you run OUTLOOK EXPRESS and you are not already connected to the Internet, the <u>DIAL-UP CONNECTION</u> box will appear. For the moment you DON'T need to go online – it's a waste of your telephone bill – so click on the <u>WORK OFFLINE</u> button. Now let's write an e-mail.

1 Click on <u>CREATE A NEW MAIL MESSAGE</u>.

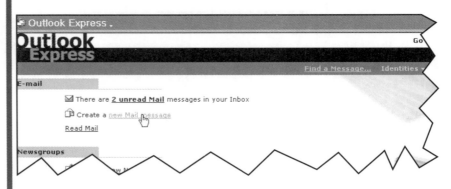

E-mail of address of the recipient.

E-mail of addresses of additional recipients (if required).

2 Enter the details as required in the <u>TO:</u>, <u>CC:</u> and <u>SUBJECT:</u> boxes. Type your message in the text area.

Subject of the e-mail.

Text area.

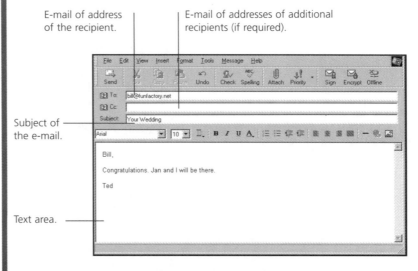

3 Click on <u>SEND</u>.

4 Click on <u>OK</u> to place your e-mail in the <u>OUTBOX</u> ready to be transmitted.

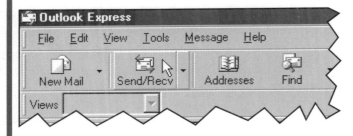

SENDING AN E-MAIL

At this point, your e-mail is now waiting in the OUTBOX to be sent. If you want to edit your message, all you have to do is click on the OUTBOX folder, which will "collapse" to show its contents. Double-click on the e-mail you want to edit and it will appear on the screen ready for you to alter. If you want to write any more e-mails you should do so while you are still offline. Now let's send your message.

1 Click on the <u>SEND/RECV</u> button.

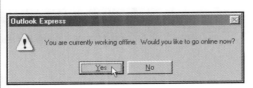

2 Click on <u>YES</u> if you want to go online. This will invoke the <u>DIAL-UP CONNECTION</u> screen.

3 To send all the e-mails that are in your <u>OUTBOX</u>, click on <u>CONNECT</u>. When the Internet connection has been made, they will be sent automatically.

RECEIVING AN E-MAIL

How do you know when somebody has sent an e-mail to you? It's easy – when you go online the main screen of Outlook Express immediately tells you if you have any mail waiting in your INBOX.

1 Click on the highlighted text telling you that you have unread mail waiting for you.

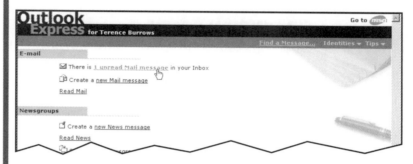

2 This opens the INBOX folder. To read the message, double-click anywhere on the line.

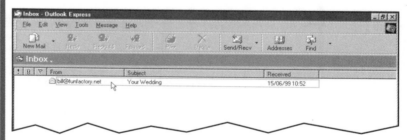

3 The message is displayed in the bottom half of the screen.

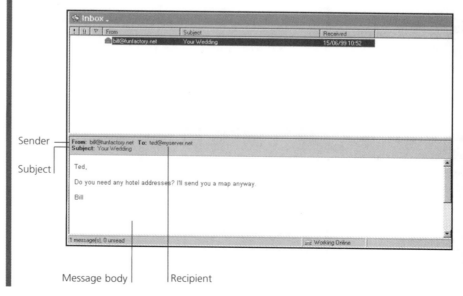

Sender

Subject

Message body   Recipient

E-MAIL AND NETIQUETTE

E-mails are extremely informal. When you compose an e-mail try to think of them as being more like extracts from a conversation rather than a traditional letter. Few experienced Netheads begin their e-mails with "Dear Fred..." and end "Yours sincerely...". At best you might get a "Hi, Fred" or just "Fred" at the start of a message – in many cases the text will get right down to business straight away. If you are dealing with large numbers of e-mails each day, then speed is of the essence (if you don't want it to completely take over your life, that is). To this end, a culture of abbreviations for oft-used phrases has emerged. These can be dropped into your e-mails at will. Some of the most commonly used acronyms are shown below. Beware of using your own abbreviations, though, unless you're really sure that the other person will understand them.

AFAIK	As far as I know	**BCNU**	Be seeing you
BST	But seriously though	**BTW**	By the way
CU	See you	**FWIW (4WIW)**	For what it's worth
FYI	For your information	**IM(NS)HO**	In my (not so) humble opinion
IMO	In my opinion	**IOW**	In other words
KISS	Keep it simple, stupid	**L8R**	Later
LOL	Laughs out loud	**MYOB**	Mind your own business
OAO	Over and out	**OIC**	Oh, I see
OTOH	On the other hand	**PITA**	Pain in the a***
ROFL	Rolls on floor laughing	**TIA**	Thanks in advance
TNX	Thanks	**WTF**	What the f***

Also widely used are emoticons (or "smilies" as they are better known). Created using punctuation keys, when looked at from the side they appear to be faces that convey different feelings.

:-)	Happy	**:-(**	Sad	**:-))**	Very happy	**:-((**	Very sad
;-)	Winking	**>:-)**	Devilishly grinning	**:-D**	Laughing	**:'-(**	Crying
:-O	Surprised	**:-|**	Unamused	**:-||**	Angry	**:-/**	Mixed feelings
:-s	Tongue-tied	**8-)**	Wears glasses	***-)**	Tired / Wasted	**:-#**	Man with beard

Finally, a general word about all forms of online interaction. There is a kind of social code at work on the Internet. This is known as "netiquette". Not only does it encourage users to be broadly polite to one another (unless riled, in which case often very aggressive "flaming" takes over), but to use the resources of the Internet with respect – for example, not wasting Internet "band width" by sending junk e-mail or uneccesarily large files. Of course, the nature of written language causes problems of its own. It can be difficult to project certain aspects of speech, such as irony or other forms of humour. And don't forget that you may be addressing a global audience – what's funny in one country may be dull, weird or downright rude in another.

REPLYING TO AN E-MAIL

If you want to reply to one of your messages you don't have to bother retyping all the address details into a new message: you just use the <u>REPLY</u> button. Another benefit of doing it this way is that the original message text is shown in the body of your own message, usually indented by the "greater than" symbol (">"). This makes the flow of conversation easier to follow – the recipient will immediately understand those parts of the original mail to which you are responding.

1 Highlight the message in the INBOX to which you want to reply. Click on <u>REPLY</u>.

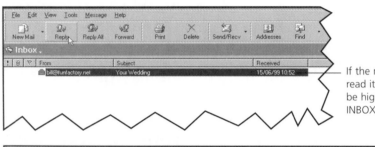

If the message is being read it will automatically be highlighted in the INBOX.

2 The original text appears in the body of the message (note the indentation). This text can be altered or added to in any way. When you have finished your reply, click on <u>SEND</u>. To transmit the message, use the instructions shown on pages 134-135.

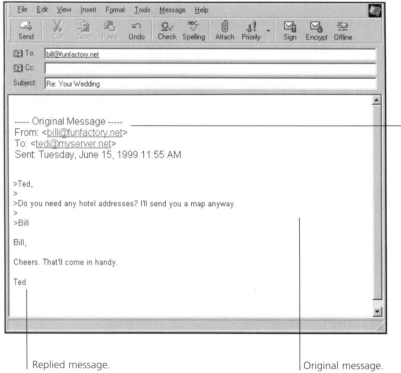

Original message header.

Replied message.

Original message.

ATTACHING FILES

As well as sending text e-mails, you can also transmit files that contain programs, images, sounds or text formatted for use with specific types of software. These files are referred to as "attachments".

1 Write your e-mail and then click on the ATTACH button.

2 The INSERT ATTACHMENT dialog box appears. Select the file you want to send with your e-mail and click on ATTACH.

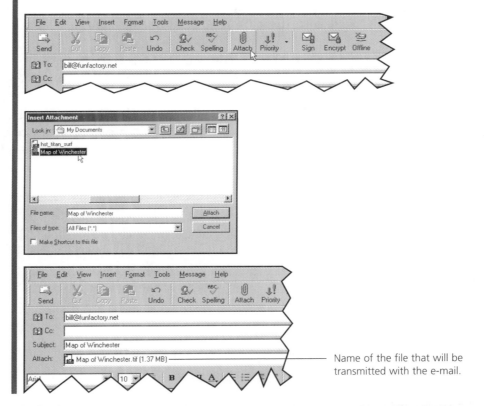

3 The file name now appears in the ATTACH: box at the top of the message window. header. Click on SEND to complete the job.

Name of the file that will be transmitted with the e-mail.

COMPRESSING FILES

One of the problems of sending files across the Internet is that it can take an eternity for them to download (and upload at the other end). A neat solution is to use a data compression program. This is a clever piece of software that scrunches the file down to a small proportion – sometimes less than five percent – of its original size. This means that it takes proportionately less time to send across the Internet, which saves you money on your telephone bill. The only consideration you have to make is that when the file gets to its destination the recipient will need a similar program to restore it to its original form. One of the most commonly used compression formats is "ZIP" (WinZip is one of the best programs for creating .zip files). This can typically compress a JPEG or GIF file to less than ten per cent of its original size.

EASIER E-MAIL

Outlook Express has many other features that will save you time and effort when sending e-mails and keeping records of your communication. For example, it includes the facility to set up address books and to filter your e-mails so that you can specify that certain types of message get delivered automatically into their own special mailboxes.

CREATING AN ADDRESS BOOK

E-mail addresses can be a pain: one letter typed out of place or in the wrong case and your mails will be "returned to sender". Luckily, Outlook Express allows you to set up an address book in your e-mail reader. This means that once an individual's details have been stored you won't ever need to enter them again. Here's one of several possible approaches to setting up an address book.

1 In the INBOX, click on a mail whose details you want to put in your address book.

2 Choose the option ADD SENDER TO ADDRESS BOOK from the TOOLS menu. Then click on ADDRESSES .

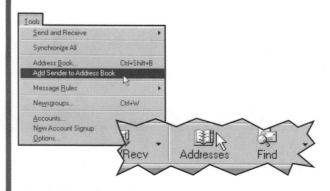

3 With the new entry highlighted click on PROPERTIES.

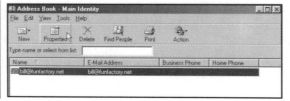

4 Click on the tabs at the top of the screen to get the right form to add different kinds of information, and click beside the category to add something there. Click on <u>OK</u> when you have finished.

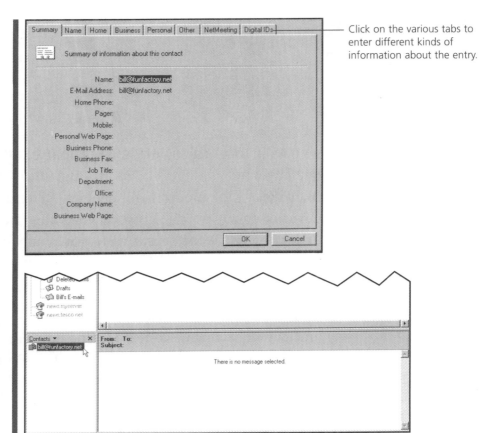

Click on the various tabs to enter different kinds of information about the entry.

5 New addresses can be displayed in the <u>CONTACT</u> box on the bottom left-hand corner of the page. Double-click on an entry to create a new readily addressed blank e-mail.

FILTERING MAIL _ □ ☒

If you reach the stage where you start to receive a large number of e-mails on a daily basis, you can easily become disorganized. One way of dealing with this problem is by filtering your mail so that it automatically goes into specially allocated mail boxes. You do this in Outlook Express by creating what are known as "Rules". By clicking on MESSAGE RULES in the TOOLS menu you will call up the NEW MAIL RULES dialog box. Here you will find options to set up specific conditions, followed by actions to take when those conditions are met. Conditions can include specific words that are displayed within the e-mail's header or body; actions can include moving or copying the file to a different folder. For example, if you set up a new mailbox folder called "Fred's E-mails", you can enter options to create a rule that says "Where the From line contains fred@myserver.net, move it to the Fred's E-mails folder". You can also use rules to effectively block incoming e-mail if you choose. For example if you are being continually bombarded with unwanted junk mail from "offers@too_good_to_refuse.com", then you can set up a rule that says "Where the From line contains offers@too_good_to_refuse.com, delete it". Thereafter any mail from that address will go straight to the recycle bin – you won't even see it.

THE WORLD WIDE WEB

The World Wide Web is the most exciting aspect of the Internet. The Web, as it's usually termed, consists of millions of electronic "pages" through which you can navigate by clicking on special "hot" links that automatically take you to a new location within the same page or to a different Web site altogether.

WHAT'S OUT THERE?

Web sites can be divided into two broad categories: business and personal. Business sites can include elaborate adverts for new technology, online newspapers and magazines, as well as shopping malls in which you can make online credit-card purchases. Personal sites are likely to be more diverse in quality and tone. They can range from personal pages about the author to sites devoted to favourite rock bands or hobbies.

The "Rough Guides" travel site

Jean-Paul Gaultier's fashion site

The New York Times Online

WEB ADDRESSES ▄ ▢ ☒

Even if you have never used the Internet, you can't have failed to notice those ubiquitous little codes beginning with http://www that you often see on advertisements or at the end of television programmes. These are web addresses. Technically known as "Uniform Resource Locators", most people simply know them as URLs. A URL is made up of three components: the protocol; the domain; and the page (which may include a file path). The first part of a Web page's URL will always begin with the letters http followed by a colon and two forward slashes. It is this code that tells your browser that it is a Web page. Since the protocol for Web sites is ALWAYS the same, to simplify matters you'll often see this part omitted when web addresses are printed (so they start just with "www"). The second part of the URL is the domain name. At its simplest, the domain tells you on whose computer the Web site appears. The third part of the URL is the page name. If this incorporates text separated by slashes you know that the page is buried in a hierarchy of folders and sub-folders. Here is an example of a typical URL.

$$\underline{\textbf{http://www}}.\underline{\textbf{yahoo.com}}\underline{\textbf{/r/cf}}$$

| Protocol | Domain | Page/path |

USING A BROWSER

To survey the wonders of the World Wide Web all you need is a piece of software called a "Web browser". Fortunately for all Windows 98 users, Internet Explorer comes as a free part of the package.

When you run Internet Explorer, it will first look to see whether or not you are online. If you aren't connect to the Internet it will automatically prompt you by launching the Windows 98 dial-up screen. When you are online, the browser will attempt to connect to its default home page, which is initially set to http://www.microsoft.com – Microsoft's home page. As you will see later, this is actually a fairly good starting point for surfing the Web since it contains many useful hyperlinks to other sites. This means that you can begin your adventures on the Web without knowing a single URL.

Navigation is really straightforward. You either click on a hyperlink within a Web page to take you somewhere else, or, if you know the URL of the site you wish to visit, all you do is position the cursor in the ADDRESS box, type over the existing URL and press the ENTER key. That's all there is to it.

INTERNET EXPLORER

To use the World Wide Web, you need a Web browser. Microsoft Internet Explorer comes as part of Windows 98. Over the next few pages you will see some of Internet Explorer's basic operating functions. Its main rival, Netscape, works in a broadly similar fashion.

HOME PAGE

The basic Internet Explorer screen can be split into six parts. The title bar tells you the name of the current Web site. The menu bar is made up of six drop-down menus that control the program's functionality. The navigation bar contains options that govern your movements around the Web. The address bar shows the URL of the current Web site. The main area of the

Title bar

Menu bar

Navigation bar

Web page URL

Web page content

Status bar

screen displays the Web page content. Finally, the Status Bar at the foot of the screen indicates how much of a Web site has been loaded – a percentage figure is displayed until it reaches 100 per cent when the Status Bar reads "Done".

Below you can find detailed descriptions of the contents of each drop-down menu and of the Navigation Bar and Address Bar. Each of these bars can be switched on or off by double-clicking on the vertical stripe at the far left of each bar. You can further maximize page space in Internet Explorer by pressing the "F11" key.

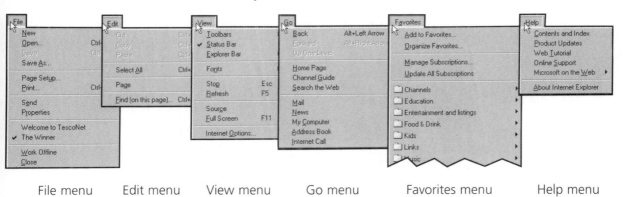

File menu   Edit menu   View menu   Go menu   Favorites menu   Help menu

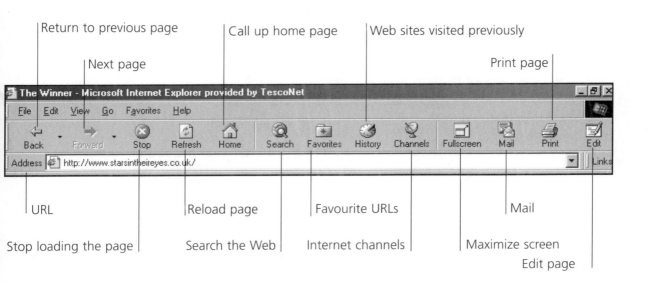

Return to previous page   Call up home page   Web sites visited previously

Next page   Print page

URL   Reload page   Favourite URLs   Mail

Stop loading the page   Search the Web   Internet channels   Maximize screen

Edit page

LET'S BROWSE!

You are now ready to get out there surfing on the World Wide Web. In no time at all you can be viewing some of the millions of fascinating sites.

THE MICROSOFT NETWORK HOME PAGE

In this example we'll run Internet Explorer and take a look at some of the options offered by the Microsoft Network's home page. This has lots of links to other interesting pages. Don't worry about whatever home page your browser loads by default – just follow the steps below.

1 Run Internet Explorer by clicking on the icon in the task bar at the foot of the screen.

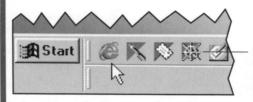

Quick Launch icons are shown along the bottom of the Windows 98 screen. You can also run the programs by double-clicking on the application itself or a desk top shortcut.

2 If you are not online you'll be prompted with the <u>CONNECT TO</u> box. If it doesn't appear, go to the <u>DIAL-UP NETWORKING</u> folder and launch the connection from there.

3 Irrespective of which Web page has already loaded, type the URL http://www.msn.com in the <u>ADDRESS</u> box.

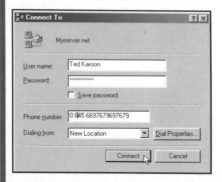

4 The MSN home page will load. Click on the main story.

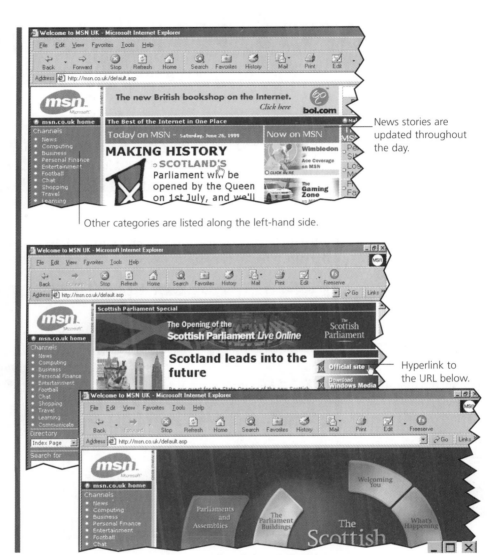

News stories are updated throughout the day.

Other categories are listed along the left-hand side.

5 The next page you see is the full story behind the headline on the previous page. Click on any of the other hyperlinks to continue surfing the Web.

Hyperlink to the URL below.

THE NETSCAPE ALTERNATIVE

Before Internet Explorer was bundled in with Windows, the most popular browser by far was Netscape Navigator. Now a part of the wider-ranging Netscape Communicator package which incorporates mail and newsgroup readers as well as Web page composition features, Navigator is still favoured by many as browser of choice. In truth, both browsers do a similar fine job, with differences being largely cosmetic. Like Internet Explorer, Netscape Communicator can be downloaded free of charge. You can get it from http://www.netscape.com.

FAVOURITE SITES

As you surf the Web you will often come across sites that you want to return to again and again. Rather than keeping a note of the URL and re-typing it each time you want to gain access, Internet Explorer allows you to store your favourite sites so that you can connect to them at the click of a button.

SAVING THOSE SITES

Storing your best-loved sites is simplicity itself using Internet Explorer's "Favorites" feature.

1 Whilst you are connected to the site you want to store, select <u>ADD TO FAVORITES</u> from the <u>FAVORITES</u> menu.

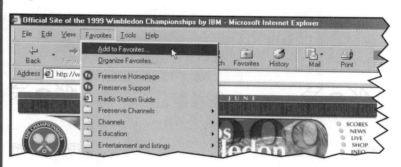

2 The <u>ADD FAVORITE</u> dialog box appears. Click on <u>CREATE IN</u>.

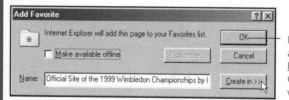

If you click on <u>OK</u>, the site will be added to the bottom of the <u>FAVORITES</u> drop-down menu. Clicking on <u>CREATE IN</u> organizes it within a folder.

3 Select a suitable category folder from the list, and click on <u>OK</u>.

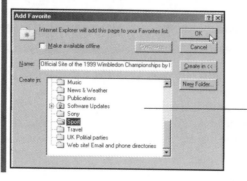

Internet Explorer is installed with a useful selection of category folders. If you want to set up a new one click on <u>NEW FOLDER</u>.

ACCESSING A "FAVORITE" SITE

As long as you are online, visiting a "favorite" site can be achieved with a couple of clicks of the mouse. To re-visit the site you have just stored, click on the <u>FAVORITES</u> menu and select <u>SPORT</u>. From the <u>SPORT</u> pop-up menu that appears, select your site. An alternative is shown at the foot of the page.

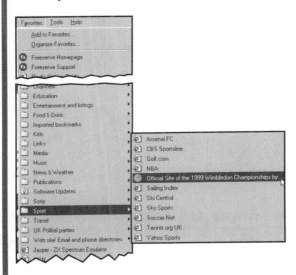

1 If you click on the FAVORITES icon in the Navigation Bar, the FAVORITES menu appears at the side of the page. Double-click on any folder to "explode" it to show the sites within. Double-click on any site to open it up.

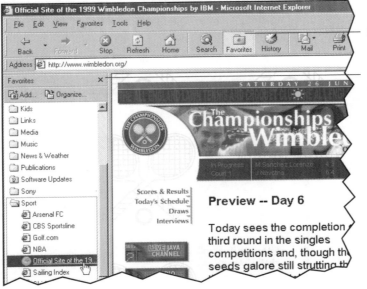

Favorites icon

Click on <u>X</u> to collapse the Favorites menu and restore the site to the full page.

SEARCH ENGINES

Clicking on "hot" links is an enjoyable way to get around the World Wide Web, but what if you want to find more specific information? The answer comes in the form of "search engines". These are Web sites in which you enter a keyword that will generate a list of sites relevant to your request.

USING A SEARCH ENGINE

There are a many different search engines from which you can choose – a list is shown on the opposite page. For this example we'll use a search engine called EXCITE to find web pages about the film *Reservoir Dogs*.

1 Type in the URL for the EXCITE search engine – http://www.excite.co.uk.

Keywords | Site range

2 Select the range of sites from the drop-down menu from which your search will be made. Type in your keyword or words and press ENTER.

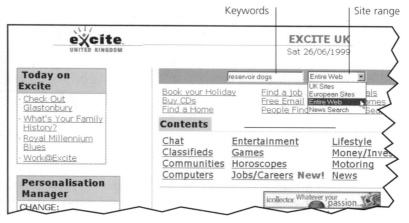

3 The EXCITE main page lists the results of your search.

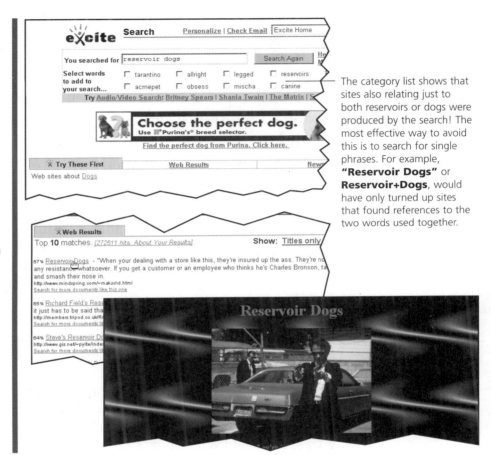

The category list shows that sites also relating just to both reservoirs or dogs were produced by the search! The most effective way to avoid this is to search for single phrases. For example, **"Reservoir Dogs"** or **Reservoir+Dogs**, would have only turned up sites that found references to the two words used together.

4 Click on any of the hyperlinks in the list to get connected to the website.

OTHER SEARCH SITES ▢▢✕

There are two distinct types of search site. Search engines use "robot" programs that constantly scour cyberspace, collecting names, locations and details about Web sites they find. These are formed into a huge database to which you connect when you make a search. The alternative is a Web directory which is a hand-built list of pages sorted into categories and a seemingly endless hierarchy of sub-categories. The main difference between the two is that search engines delve deeper into cyberspace and are more up-to-date, whereas directories offer you a far more focussed search.

ALTAVISTA	http://www.altavista.com	**EXCITE**	http://excite.com
FREEPAGES	http://www.freepages.co.uk	**GOTO**	http://www.goto.com
HOTBOT	http://www.hotbot.com	**INFOSEEK**	http://www.infoseek.com
LOOKSMART	http://www.looksmart.com	**LYCOS**	http://www.lycos.com
SNAP	http://www.snap.com	**WEBCRAWLER**	http://www.webcrawler.com
YAHOO!	http://www.yahoo.com	**YELL**	http://www.yell.com

DDING PLUG-INS

With all aspects of the Internet developing at a rapid rate, sometimes Internet Explorer needs a helping hand to deal with the most advanced multimedia sites. This usually comes in the form of a "plug-in".

WHAT ARE PLUG-INS?

Plug-ins are small programs that add functionality to your Web browser. They are needed where a site does much more than simply display text and images, such as playing sounds and videos, or displaying animations or three-dimensional models.

When Internet Explorer requires a plug-in it will not only tell you about it, but will also provide a hyperlink connection to a site from which you can download that plug-in.

PLUG-INS OR VIEWERS?

A plug-in enables a sound or image to be displayed within Internet Explorer's own window. A different kind of add-on – usually referred to as a "viewer" – is a separate program that opens its own window to play or display sounds and images. These programs can function independently from the browser, but are usually "kick-started" by an instruction from a website.

REALAUDIO

One of the most useful viewers is RealPlayer, a program that can play streamed audio and video from the Web. This means that sounds and video clips can be played as they are being down-loaded. You can obtain the RealPlayer software from http://www.realaudio.com.

MP3

The most recent buzz in the Internet music world is a new file format called MP3, which can allow near-CD-quality music to be downloaded from the Internet. Using an incredible degree of data compression, a three-minute stereo pop song can be reduced to around three megabytes of data. Where once it might have taken an hour or more to download such a file, it should now take less than ten minutes.

To play MP3 files you need an MP3 player. One of the most popular players is Winamp. Not only can this play MP3 files, but numerous other audio formats. It can be downloaded from http://www.winamp.com.

Counter

Track details

Mono/stereo indicator

Meters

Transport controls

Preamplifier to boost or cut the overall volume.

Ten-band graphic equalizer provides fine tone control.

VIDEO FORMATS

The main difficulty in making the most sophisticated plug-ins do their work is the speed at which we are connected to the Internet. This is especially true of video clips where, even if you have a 56K modem, download times are long and the picture quality rather jerky. In short, a one-minute video clip will be around three megabytes in size. It'll take at least ten minutes to download and when it arrives it won't look too fantastic.

There are three commonly used file formats. They are: MPEG, whose files can be recognized by the extensions .mpg, .mpe or .mpeg; QUICKTIME, which was created by Apple but is now well established across all platforms (with the extensions .mov and .qt); and the lesser-used VIDEO FOR WINDOWS, which uses the file extension .avi.

VIDEO PLUG-INS AND VIEWERS

To see and hear a video file you need a software player capable of working with the appropriate format. ActiveMovie, which is loaded with Internet Explorer, is both a browser plug-in and an independent viewer. Although this software can read the three main formats, it is only completely reliable for reading .avi files. A better alternative is to download a piece of shareware called Net Toob, which can not only read numerous video and audio formats but also provide streaming for MPEG movies (http://www.nettoob.com).

ANIMATION

In recent times, animation has exploded on the Web, largely a result of the two Macromedia plug-ins, ShockWave and Flash. ShockWave allows browsers to view Web sites that feature sophisticated animations created with Macromedia Director. A widely used multimedia program, Director can integrate images, videos and text to create superb animations. The Flash plug-in creates simpler animations.

These two excellent plug-ins can be easily obtained from Macromedia (http://www.macromedia.com). Some interesting uses of both Flash and ShockWave plug-ins can be found on http://www.shockwave.com, Macromedia's site devoted to showing off their product's potential.

Each button on this ShockWave page creates a new animation in the centre screen.

JAVA AND ACTIVE-X

Two names that you are certain to come across in relation to multimedia on the Web are "Java" and "ActiveX". JAVA is a programming language developed by Sun computers which enables Web pages to contain special in-built programs called "applets". These programs can make static Web pages more lively or interactive. Similar is Microsoft's own ActiveX, which adds functionality to Internet Explorer. ActiveX was designed to work as an extension of the Windows operating system. If you encounter a Web site that contains an ActiveX program you will usually be given a warning with an option not to download. JAVA also has a scripting language that can be incorporated into HTML. Called "JAVSCRIPT", these routines are more convenient but much slower than the applets.

THE THIRD DIMENSION

Virtual Reality Modelling Languages (VRML) are incredible plug-ins that allow you to see the same image from different angles either by moving the cursor around on the screen or by clicking on a control panel. Imagine, for example, that you see an image of a room from a perspective as if you had just walked through the door. By dragging the mouse to the top of the picture the image slowly pans upwards to the ceiling.

VRML plug-ins are usually given the suffix .wrl. Two of the most popular examples are WIRL (downloadable from http://www.platinum.com) and Superscape's Viscape (http://www.superscape.com). The latter can be seen in the example below which shows four views of the same car taken at different points in its rotation.

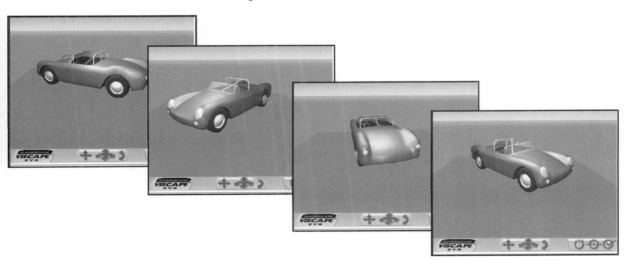

CREATING YOUR HOME PAGE

With free Web space now offered as standard by almost every ISP, any Internet user can set up and maintain his or her own set of home pages.

HTML OR INTERACTIVE SOFTWARE?

Web pages are constructed using a programming language called HTML. This is extremely easy to learn, and doesn't really require any traditional computer programming skills. However, it's possible to bypass this process by using interactive software that allows you to position text and images on a page and then automatically generate "hidden" HTML code. Internet Explorer has its own in-built web publishing program called FrontPage Express. Here is a very simple example using this program. Begin by opening FrontPage Express.

1 Enter some text in the untitled new page.

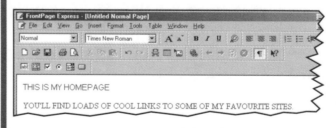

2 To alter the size of the text, highlight your selection and choose an option from the drop-down menu.

Header 1 is the largest size.

3 To add a picture, choose <u>IMAGE</u> from the <u>INSERT</u> menu. In the <u>IMAGE</u> dialog box click on <u>BROWSE</u> and select the desired file.

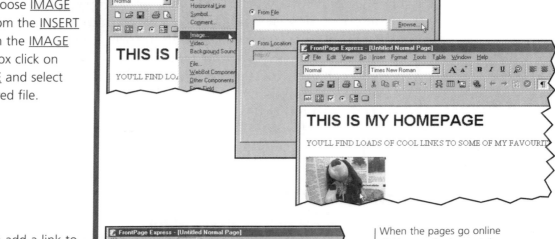

4 To add a link to the image, click on the image and then choose <u>HYPERLINK</u> from the <u>INSERT</u> menu. Enter the URL for your link and then click on <u>OK</u>.

When the pages go online clicking on the image takes you to the specified URL.

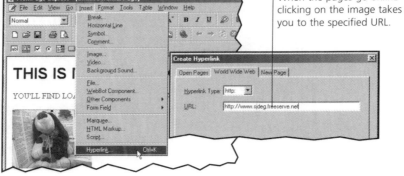

5 You can set up an e-mail link in a similar way. Highlight some text and choose <u>HYPERLINK</u> from the <u>INSERT</u> menu. Change the <u>HYPERLINK TYPE</u> from "<u>http:</u>" to "<u>mailto:</u>". Enter the e-mail address and click on <u>OK</u>.

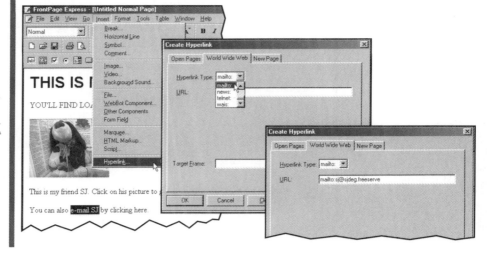

PUBLISHING YOUR WEB PAGE

For the rest of the world to view your Web pages they have to be on your ISP's Web server. It's easy to upload your pages using FrontPage Express. The only information you need is the location on your ISP's server where they will reside. You may have to call your ISP to find out this address.

Before you publish, make sure that your entry-level page is correctly named "index.html". This ensures that when anyone types in your basic URL without the page name or path – for example, http://www.altavista.com – this is the page that will appear.

1 Click on SAVE AS in the FILE menu. In the SAVE AS dialog box, enter the PAGE TITLE and the PAGE LOCATION. Click on OK.

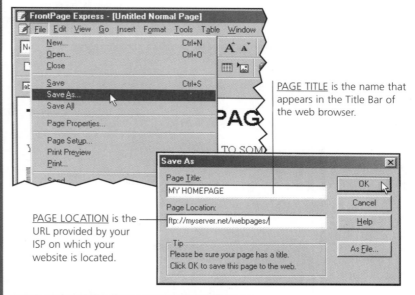

PAGE TITLE is the name that appears in the Title Bar of the web browser.

PAGE LOCATION is the URL provided by your ISP on which your website is located.

2 If you are offline, FrontPage Express will call prompt a connection. Follow the steps of the WEB PUBLICATION WIZARD until all of your files have been uploaded.

REFERENCE SECTION

10

The final section contains basic information like how to install Windows 98 or other programs, and how to print hard copies of your work. You'll also find a comprehensive list of keyboard shortcuts to help you work more efficiently, as well some tips on what to do when things go wrong. The final few pages of the book comprise a glossary of technical terms you'll often hear uttered in the PC world.

INSTALLING WINDOWS 98

In the unlikely event that Windows 98 didn't come already loaded on your PC, or if you are upgrading from a previous version of Windows, you will have to install it yourself. Don't worry, the process is just about as automatic as it could be – all you have to do is click your way through a few screens.

SYSTEM REQUIREMENTS

Before you get started, you need to ensure that your PC meets the basic requirements to run Windows 98. It doesn't especially need to be the last word in technical development, although some of the latest programs you may want to run within Windows 98 will be more demanding. At its most basic, your PC needs to have a bare minimum of:

- 486 processor
- A minimum of 16MB of RAM (32 MB is preferable).
- At least 250 MB hard disk space.
- A CD-ROM drive (or a DVD-ROM drive).

THE INSTALLATION PROCESS

1. Begin by inserting the Windows 98 Installation disk into your PC's CD-ROM drive. You should receive a message box asking you if you would like to upgrade to Windows 98. Click on <u>YES</u>. Move on to step 3.

2. If you are upgrading from older versions of Windows and the message box above does not appear, click on <u>START</u> and then choose <u>RUN</u> from the Start Menu.

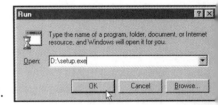

The <u>RUN</u> dialog box will appear. Enter <u>D:\setup.exe</u> (this is assuming that your CD-ROM is drive <u>D:</u> – if it isn't, change it to the correct letter). Click on <u>OK</u>.

3. The <u>WINDOWS 98 SETUP</u> screen starts up and announces its intention to do a quick check on your PC for any problems that might lay ahead. If it finds anything strange it should fix it. Click on <u>CONTINUE</u>.

4. If Windows 98 finds anything wrong with your PC's hard disk it will try to fix it. At this point it will also give you a reasonably accurate estimate of how long the installation process will take to complete. Click on <u>CONTINUE</u>.

5. The <u>WINDOWS 98 SETUP WIZARD APPEARS</u>. The first page is merely a license agreement. Click on <u>NEXT</u>.

6. The Windows 98 Setup Wizard asks you if you want to save your existing MS-DOS or Windows systems. On balance, it's probably a good idea to enter <u>YES</u> at this point since it at least gives the option of uninstalling Windows 98 if you should want to. Click on <u>NEXT</u>.

7. The Windows 98 Setup Wizard asks you for the country you live in so that it knows which are the relevant default Internet Channels to set up for you. Click on <u>NEXT</u>.

8. The installer will now create an emergency start-up disk for you, so insert a blank floppy disk into drive A: (your floppy drive). Click on <u>NEXT</u>. When it finishes its writing, the disk will automatically eject.

9. The Windows 98 Setup Wizard finally begins the laborious process of copying files and configuring your hard disk. At this point you can disappear for a cup of coffee for at least a half an hour – there's nothing at all for you to do. When you return to your PC, click on <u>FINISH</u> to complete the installation and watch Windows 98 burst into life.

INSTALLING PROGRAMS

Adding and removing programs is usually a pretty straightforward business using Windows 98. You'll find that most of the popular programs have their own self-installation processes. All you have to do is insert the CD and click on the dialog boxes that follow. If not, Windows 98 has its own functions for installing and uninstalling programs.

INSTALLING FROM A CD-ROM

Here is a typical example of installing a program – in this case, the graphics software CorelDraw 7. As soon as you insert the CD into your drive, CorelDraw's installer takes over.

1 Click on the INSTALL COREL-DRAW 7 option.

2 Follow the steps through the COREL SETUP WIZARD, completing the boxes where necessary. Click on NEXT to move to each subsequent box.

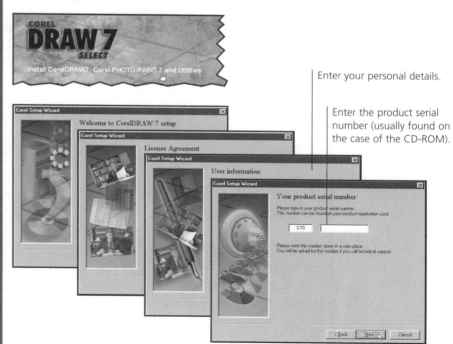

Enter your personal details.

Enter the product serial number (usually found on the case of the CD-ROM).

3 On the screens that follow you can specify your installation options. As before, click on NEXT to move on.

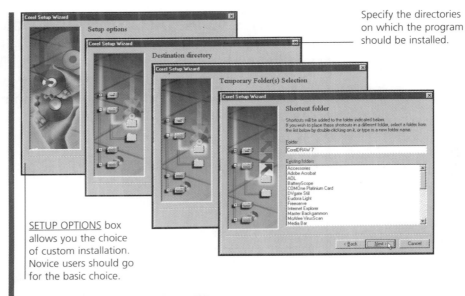

Specify the directories on which the program should be installed.

SETUP OPTIONS box allows you the choice of custom installation. Novice users should go for the basic choice.

4 The COREL SETUP WIZARD is finally ready to install its files. Click on NEXT.

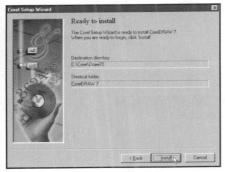

5 A progress bar shows how much of the process is complete. The INSTALLATION COMPLETE box will appear at the end of this process. Click on OK. You may need to restart Windows 98 before you can use the program.

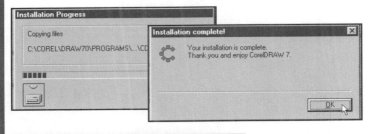

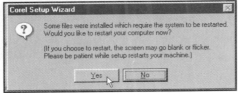

WINDOWS 98 INSTALLATION FUNCTION

If the program you want to install doesn't offer an automatic installation feature – as may be the case with some programs that can be downloaded from the Internet –you should be able to use Windows 98's Add/Remove Programs function, which can be found in the Control Panel.

1 Click on START, and select SETTINGS from the START menu. Choose CONTROL PANEL from the menu.

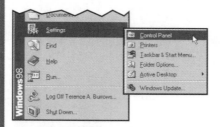

2 In the CONTROL PANEL, double-click on ADD/ REMOVE PROGRAMS.

3 In ADD/REMOVE PROPERTIES, click on the INSTALL/UNINSTALL tab. Click on INSTALL.

4 The next screen looks for a CD or floppy disk ready to install a program. If it can't find one, you have to enter the relevant name and drive in the RUN INSTALLATION PROGRAM dialog box that follows. Then click on FINISH.

Enter drive, file path and name of installation program.

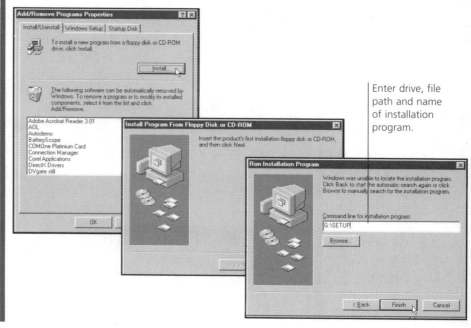

REMOVING PROGRAMS

Windows 98 views the addition and removal of programs as being two sides of the same process; consequently they function in much the same way. Let's look at an example of removing a program which has been installed using the Add/Remove Programs function. Follow steps 1 and 2 from across the page.

1 In ADD/REMOVE PROGRAM PROPERTIES, click on the tab marked INSTALL/UNINSTALL. Use the scroll bars or arrows to find the program you wish to remove. Highlight the name and then click on ADD/REMOVE.

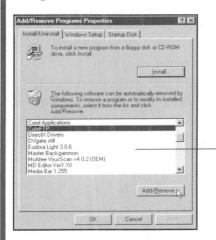

List of programs loaded on this PC's hard disk that Windows 98's Add/Remove Programs functon can uninstall.

2 In the SELECT UNINSTALL-METHOD box, click on AUTOMATIC and then NEXT. In the PERFORM UNINSTALL dialog box, click on NEXT. The program will now be removed.

WHY UNINSTALL?

Unless you have a particular bent towards techno-masochism, whenever you install a program you are generally only aware of the application file itself. This is the .exe file, which you double-click on (or create a shortcut from) to launch the software. However, each installation also buries away numerous other mysterious bits and pieces – things without which the program won't run. Therefore, removing a program is not simply a case of dragging the .exe file it into the Recycle Bin. You *could* do it that way, but that would leave behind all the associated files to clog up your PC. Using ADD/REMOVE PRO-GRAMS (or an alternative piece of software) removes all traces of the program.

PRINTING

For those of you who didn't get a printer bundled in with the price of your PC, you'll need to get one if you want to create even a hard copy of a word-processed letter. The next few pages show you the basics of printing.

INSTALLING YOUR PRINTER

Before you can make your printer work, it needs to be connected to your PC and switched on, and then it has to be installed by Windows 98. The Add Printer function stores profiles of most of the most popular models on the market.

1 Click on START, and select SETTINGS from the START menu. Choose PRINTERS from the menu.

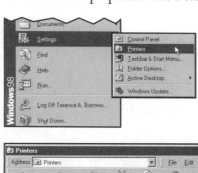

2 In the PRINTERS window, double-click on ADD PRINTER.

3 In the first page of the ADD PRINTER WIZARD, click on NEXT. The subsequent page asks if the printer is local or a part of a network. For almost all domestic uses choose LOCAL. Click on NEXT.

If the printer is connected directly to your PC, then it is a LOCAL PRINTER.

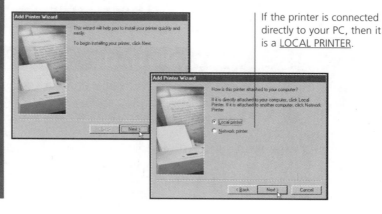

4 Use the scroll bars or arrows to select the manufacturer and model of the printer you have connected. Click on NEXT.

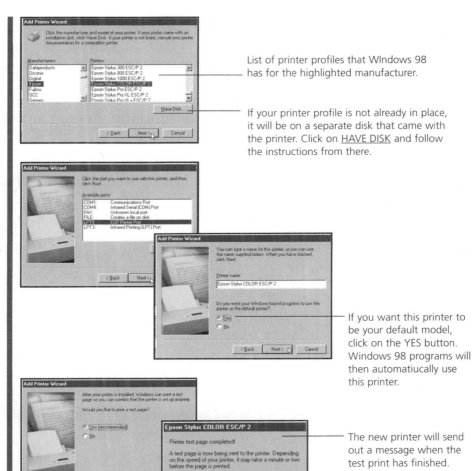

List of printer profiles that WIndows 98 has for the highlighted manufacturer.

If your printer profile is not already in place, it will be on a separate disk that came with the printer. Click on HAVE DISK and follow the instructions from there.

5 Select the port you want to use with your printer. It is more than likely to be LPT1. Click on NEXT. The screen that follows gives you the option of renaming the printer. Click on NEXT.

If you want this printer to be your default model, click on the YES button. Windows 98 programs will then automatiucally use this printer.

5 Before the printer is fully set up, it's a good idea to accept a test print to ensure that it's working properly. To end the installation, click on FINISH.

The new printer will send out a message when the test print has finished.

6 When the set-up is complete, the new printer will have its own icon in the PRINTERS window.

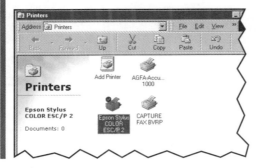

PRINTING A DOCUMENT

Once your printer is set up, getting it to print a hard copy should be a doddle. The basic outlines are shown below, although the options will vary depending both on the type of printer you are using and the program from which you are printing. Generally speaking, though, to print a document you select the <u>PRINT</u> option from the <u>FILE</u> menu (or use the shortcut <u>CTRL+P</u>).

1 Choose <u>PRINT</u> from the <u>FILE</u> menu.

2 The <u>PRINT</u> dialog box appears. Choose your settings and click on <u>OK</u>.

Default printer appears. Click on the arrow for a list of other valid printer options.

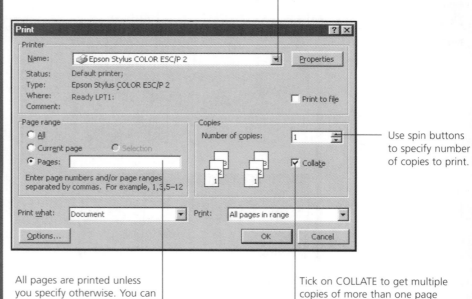

Use spin buttons to specify number of copies to print.

All pages are printed unless you specify otherwise. You can enter pages ranges in here.

Tick on COLLATE to get multiple copies of more than one page sorted in sequence.

PRINT MANAGEMENT

You can check the progress of documents that you have "sent" to the printer in the printer's own window. In most situations this should open automatically when you start printing. If it doesn't, all you have to do is double-click on the printer's icon in the Printers Control Panel folder.

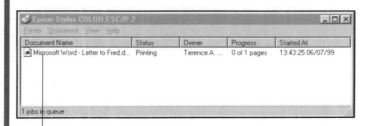

To pause or cancel the printing, right-click on the document name and select <u>PAUSE PRINTING</u> or <u>CANCEL PRINTING</u> from the drop-down menu

DRAG-AND-DROP PRINTING

Printing using the program menus is a good way of working when you have the documents open. However, if you have a document which is already written that you want to print, you needn't trouble yourself relaunching the program just for that. You can use the drag-and-drop technique. This is especially useful if you have a large number of documents to be printed in this way. For it to work you need both document and printer icon to be accessible in open windows.

1 Click and hold on the document. Now drag it out of its window and drop it on the printer icon within the <u>PRINTERS</u> window. The document will now be sent to the printer.

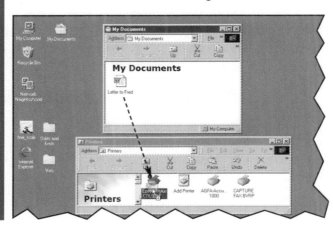

EVEN SMARTER DRAG-AND-DROP METHOD

For an even more sophisticated take on drag-and-drop printing, you can set up a shortcut icon to your printer on the desktop. This means that you don't even have to go to the trouble of opening the Printers window.

1 Click and hold on the document. Now you simply drag-and-drop into the printer icon.

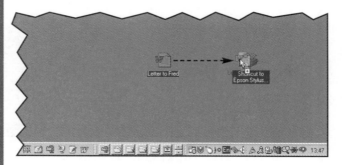

ALL ABOUT FONTS

If you're not familiar with the term, a "font" refers to the style of lettering or printing. This text is being printed in a font called "Book Antiqua"; the heading at the start of this paragraph is called "Frutiger Black". There are many thousands of fonts in existence. Here are a few examples of fonts that come ready loaded with Windows 98.

COPPERPLATE

DAUPHIN

LUCINDA HANDWRITING

POSTER BODONI

You can find out which fonts are already loaded on your PC by looking inside the <u>FONTS</u> folder, which you can access from the <u>CONTROL PANEL</u>.

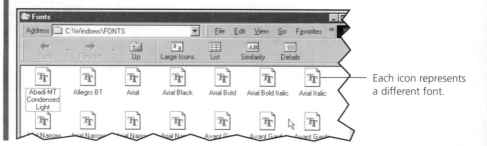

Each icon represents a different font.

WHAT DOES IT LOOK LIKE?

One of the problems with dealing with large numbers of fonts is that, unless you are a graphic designer, you are unlikely to know one font from another by name. Luckily, each font also has its own window. If you double-click on any of the icons in the Fonts folder you will be able to see how the font looks.

Font name

Option to print out font

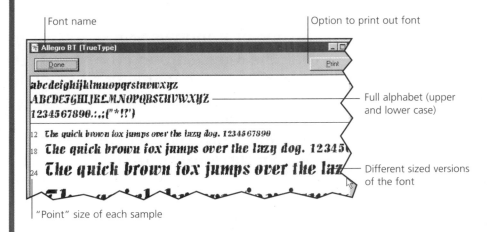

Full alphabet (upper and lower case)

Different sized versions of the font

"Point" size of each sample

LOADING FONTS

You can add as many extra fonts as you like. You can often buy bundled versions from software suppliers, or even download some free copies from the Internet. To add a new font, you can use the Fonts window. This example loads a new version of a font called "Verdana" from a floppy disk.

1 In the FONTS window, choose INSTALL NEW FONT from the FILE MENU. In the ADD FONTS dialog box select and highlight the font to be copied and click on OK.

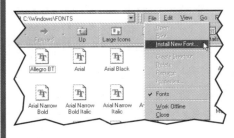

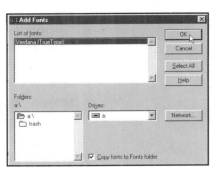

KEYBOARD SHORTCUTS

Although the mouse is without question a wonderful tool, there are numerous occasions when it's quicker to use one of Windows 98's keyboard shortcuts than to drag the mouse around the screen. Of course, the downside is that you have to learn them first. Here are the shortcuts that you are most likely to find useful.

GENERAL WINDOWS 98 SHORTCUTS

The shortcuts listed below should be good for all Windows 98 functions as well as most of the popular commercial programs designed to operate under Windows 98.

Cancel	Esc
Choose command	Alt+underlined letter
Close window/program	Alt+F4
Command prompt boot up	F8 (at Windows 98 logo)
Copy	Ctrl+C
Cut	Ctrl+X
Delete	Del key
Delete (not to Recycle Bin)	Shift+Del
Find file/folder	F3
Help	F1
Paste	Ctrl+V
Properties	Alt+Enter
Refresh	F5
Rename file/folder	F2
Screen capture	Print Scrn key
Screen capture (active window)	Alt+Print Scrn
Shortcut menu	Shift+F10
Shut down	Alt+F4 (all windows closed)
Start menu	Ctrl+Esc (or Windows key)

Step-by-step startup	**Shift+F8 (on startup beep)**
Switch programs	**Alt+Tab**
System menu	**Alt+hyphen (-)**
Undo	**Ctrl+Z**

WINDOWS EXPLORER AND MY COMPUTER

The following keyboard shortcuts can be used with Windows Explorer. Most can also be used with My Computer (those that can't are marked with an asterisk).

Back	**Alt+left arrow**
Bypass autoplay on CD	**Hold shift while inserting CD**
Close	**Alt+F4**
Close	
Collapse folder *	**Left arrow**
Collapse selected folder *	**Num Lock+hyphen(-)**
Copy selected items	**Ctrl+C**
Cut selected items	**Ctrl+X**
Delete (no Recycle Bin)	**Shift+del**
Expand folder *	**Right arrow**
Find	**F3**
Forward	**Alt+right arrow**
Paste	**Ctrl+V**
Properties	**Shift+Enter**
Refresh	**F5**
Rename	**F2**
Select all	**Ctrl+A**
Switch between panes *	**F6**
Move up a folder level	**Backspace**

INTERNET EXPLORER

These keyboard shortcuts can be used while browsing the World Wide Web with Internet Explorer.

Collapse toolbars	**F11**
Go to new location	**Ctrl+O**
Go to selected link	**Enter**
Move backward through links	**Shift+Tab**

INTERNET EXPLORER (continued)

Move backward through frames	**Shift+Ctrl+Tab**
Move forward through frames	**Ctrl+Tab**
Move forward through links	**Tab**
Move to end of document	**End**
Move to top of document	**Home**
Next page	**Alt+right arrow**
Open a new window	**Crtl+N**
Previous page	**Alt+left arrow**
Print page or frame	**Ctrl+P**
Refresh Web page	**F5**
Scroll down	**Down arrow**
Scroll down in large increments	**Page down**
Scroll up	**Up arrow**
Scroll up in large increments	**Page up**
Shortcut menu for link	**Shift+F10**
Stop downloading page	**Esc**

DIALOG BOXES

The keyboard shortcuts listed below are for navigating around dialog boxes.

Cancel without saving	**Esc**
Tick on/off	**Spacebar**
Select option	**Alt+underlined letter**
Click on default option	**Enter**
Click slected button	**Spacebar**
Move cursor to end of line	**End**
Move cursor to start of line	**Home**
Open drop-down list	**Alt+down arrow**
Select next option	**Tab**
Move to parent folder	**Backspace**
Move slider	**left or right arrows**
Select higher lower values	**up or down arrows**
Tab (next)	**Ctrl+Tab**
Tab (previous)	**Ctrl+Shift+Tab**

WINDOWS KEYBOARDS

If you have a "Microsoft Natural Keyboard" (you'll be able to tell because it has a special Windows key) you will be able to use these extra keyboard functions.

Sequence through Taskbar buttons	**Windows+Tab**
Find files/folders	**Windows+F**
Help	**Windows+F1**
Minimize or restore all windows	**Windows+D**
Run program	**Windows+R**
System properties	**Windows+break**
Undo minimize all windows	**Shift+Windows+M**
Windows Explorer	**Windows+E**

DRAG AND DROP

Although we didn't touch on this in the body of the book, you can also use shortcut keys for drag-and-drop functions. In most of these instances, you have to hold down a key BEFORE you click, hold and drag.

Cancel drag-and-drop function	**Esc**
Copy the files being dragged	**Ctrl and then drag**
Create shortcut to dragged item	**Ctrl+Shift and then drag**
Move the files being dragged	**Alt and then drag**

TROUBLESHOOTING

We all know that PCs are wonderful things, don't we? Frankly, that can easily slip the mind on those days when everything seems to running at half speed, the printer keeps jamming, the monitor is flickering…. We've all been victims to these techno-quirks, but the good news is that the majority can be sorted out quite easily. Here are some troubleshooting tips.

TROUBLE WITH THE MOUSE

- Check that it's plugged in properly – if the connection is loose the mouse may only work intermittently.
- Check that Windows 98 is configured for the correct type of mouse. It may be necessary to add a new driver using the ADD NEW HARD WARE control panel and the CD or disk that came with the mouse.
- If the mouse buttons seem to be working in reverse order, go to the MOUSE functions in the CONTROL PANEL – it can switch the mouse buttons between left and right as required.
- If the movement is jerky, the mouse may be clogged up. Remove the ball and clean the insides with a cotton wool bud.

TROUBLE WITH KEYBOARDS

- Check the connections.
- Check that nothing's been spilled over it. If it has, take the action outlined below.
- If the wrong letters start appearing on the screen, you need to look at the KEYBOARD function within the Control Panel. You'll probably find that it's set to the wrong type of keyboard or language.
- If the computer makes a continuous beeping sound, check that there is nothing leaning on the keyboard.
- If you've just poured coffee over the keyboard, disconnect the keyboard from the computer. Clean the affected areas with cold water and then dry them off with a paper towel. Avoid the temptation to use a hot air dryer since this can damage the circuitry and melt the plastic. Ensure that it's dry before you try to plug it in again.

TROUBLE WITH PRINTERS
- If it's dead, check the connections, switch it off and restart it.
- If an inkjet printer produces blurred or lined results, clean the print heads. Check that you are using the correct paper and settings.

TROUBLE WITH MONITORS
- If it seems to be dead, check the connections to the power supply and the system unit. Check that the brightness control has not been switched to complete darkness or zero contrast.
- If the Desktop "disappears" off the edge of the edge of the screen, use the vertical and horizontal adjustments to centre the picture.
- If the colours on the screen seem strange, check that the unit is not too close to a magnetic source, such as a loudspeaker.
  If your monitor has a "degauss" button, try that. Also check the cable linking the monitor to the system unit.

TROUBLE WITH HARD DISKS
- If your hard disk is full, uninstall unwanted software (this builds up – especially if you regularly install magazine freebies); delete temporary files using Disk Cleanup; Use a compression program like Windows 98's DriveSpace 3; if you haven't already done so, consider converting your drive to FAT32.
- If your hard disk seems to be working all the time, you may be running low on RAM and so Windows is using space on the hard drive as "virtual memory". If this happens persistently, add more RAM.
- If files claim suddenly to be corrupt, run ScanDisk with the parameters set to <u>AUTOMATICALLY FIX ERRORS</u>.
- If you've accidentally erased a file, try going to the Recycle Bin and using <u>RESTORE</u> to bring it back; use a recovery program like Norton Utilities to "undelete" the file.

TROUBLE WITH WINDOWS
- If Windows claims that files are missing, restart your system using the "boot disk" you made during the installation, or reinstall Windows 98 from your original CD-ROM.
- If after uninstalling a program, others stop working, reinstall the program and then uninstall it using the <u>ADD/REMOVE PROGRAMS</u> function; copy missing files from the Recycle Bin or their original disks.

# LOSSARY

If you are new to Windows 98 (or even PCs), you are certain to come across key words or phrases that leave you absolutely baffled. This is not too surprising since computer experts *love* to communicate using technical jargon. In this section you'll find simple and succinct descriptions that will help you crack some of these strange and mysterious secret codes.

ACTIVE DESKTOP
A feature of Windows 98 that allows Internet content to be shown on the desktop and updated automatically in the background.

ACTIVE WINDOW
The last window that you clicked on, making it in effect "live". The active window is always on top of the other open windows – any keys that you press will affect this window and no others.

ACCESS PROVIDER
A company that sells the facility to connect to the Internet.

ALT
A key usually found alongside the space bar which is used in conjunction with other keys to perform tasks. For example, the command <u>ALT + F4</u> tells you to hold down the "ALT" key while you press "F4"" – this instruction closes down windows or programs.

APPLICATION
An alternative name for a computer program.

ASCII
An acronym for "American Standard Code for Information Interchange". Pronounced "askey", ASCII is a standardized way of converting text into a format that can be then interpreted by any computer. It is also sometimes referred to as "plain text".

ATTACHMENT
A file of any type or format which is hooked onto an e-mail message and delivered at the same time.

BACKUP
A second copy of a computer file or program. If you're new to using computers, here is the first rule of survival: ALWAYS MAKE BACKUPS OF IMPORTANT DATA. Your computer's hard disk has not been designed to live forever – when it dies make sure your work doesn't go with it.

BAUD
The speed at which a *modem* can transfer data, measured in events per second (not, as is often suggested, bits – binary digits – per second).

BROWSER
A computer program that lets you view Web pages from the Internet. The two most commonly used browsers are Microsoft's Internet Explorer (which comes as a part of Windows 98) and Netscape's Navigator (now part of the Communicator package). Browsers can also handle other areas of Internet activity such as e-mail and newsgroups.

BUG
A program error that sometimes causes the computer to crash.

BYTE
The amount of storage a computer requires to hold a single character such as a letter or number.

CASE-SENSITIVE
The difference between capital and lower-case letters. E-mail addresses are sensitive in this way – for example, fredsmith@fishbone.co.uk would NOT necessarily receive mail that was sent to FredSmith@Fishbone.co.uk.

CD-ROM
An acronym that stands for Compact Disc Read-Only Memory. A CD-ROM looks like a regular music CD but contains computer software or files, rather than music. It's also possible to store your own files on CDs using a CD writer and special software.

CLICK

A single push and release of one of the buttons on the mouse.

CLIPBOARD

A temporary storage space that keeps track of words or pictures that have been cut or copied. They can then be accessed later and then pasted into other documents.

COMMAND

A term describing any option found on a Windows 98 drop-down menu.

CONTROL PANEL

A Windows 98 panel in which the user can personalize his or her computer. You can get to the Control Panel by clicking on the Windows 98 <u>Start</u> button, selecting the <u>Settings</u> option and then choosing <u>Control Panel</u> from the menu.

CPU

Acronym for the "Central Processing Unit", the microchip that makes your computer work.

CRASH

An error that prevents the computer working. A crash can be a result of a program error or software conflicts which require the computer to be restarted. Hardware crashes are a result of physically damaged components.

CTRL

The "Control" key which is used in conjunction with other keys to perform tasks. For example, the command <u>CTRL + Z</u> tells you to hold down the "CTRL" key while you press "Z" – this is the "undo" instruction.

CURSOR

The small vertical blinking line that appears on the screen that tells you where the next letter you type will appear.

CYBERSPACE

A term, originally coined by Sci-fi author William Gibson in his novel "Neuromancer", which is now used to describe all aspects of life on the Internet.

DATA COMPRESSION

The reduction in size of a computer file so that it can be archived or sent with greater speed across the Internet.

DESKTOP

The "active" area on the screen in which you can arrange the icons that represent programs or files, or double-click on them to make them work.

DIALOG BOX

A window that asks you to supply specific information to make a program work in the desired way.

DOCUMENT

A file containing information created or altered by a program. A document can contain text, pictures or sounds.

DOUBLE-CLICK

Pushing and releasing the left buttons on the mouse twice in quick succession.

DOWNLOADING

The process of transferring files or software from a remote computer or a web site to your own. The reverse is "uploading" which have to do when you make your own Web pages live.

DRAG AND DROP

A simple mouse manoeuvre used to move or copy files from one area to another. You first point at the object then press and hold the mouse button while you "drag" the object to the desired location before finally releasing the button to "drop" the object.

E-MAIL

Electronic mail. A system that allows computers connected to the Internet to exchange text messages.

FAQ

Acronym for "Frequently Asked Questions". A list of common questions usually found on *newsgroups* or *Web sites*, so that newcomers can avoid repeatedly asking the same questions.

FAT32

FAT is the cronym for "File Allocation Table". A stable stored on computer disk that tells the computer where to find the data it contains.

FILE

A collection of data on a computer disk.

FLAMING

The practice of sending an offensive or abusive e-mail or newsgroup posting. Usually served as a response rather than to initiate an argument.

FOLDER

A user-defined area in which files can be stored and organized so they can be easily found at a later date. Folders can appear at multiple levels, ie, a folder can contain many other folders, each of which can also contain many folders.

FONT

A term that describes different styles of lettering.

FORMAT

The preparation of a computer disk of any kind so that files can be written to them. Beware! Formatting a disk erases any existing data.

FREEWARE

Software distributed via the Internet that you can download free of charge.

FUNCTION KEYS

The line of keys at the top of the keyboard marked F1, F2 and so forth. They are often used as shortcut keys, although their exact use differs depending on the program being used.

GIGABYTE (G, GB, GIG)

Measurement of disk space which is roughly one billion bytes.

HARD DISK

The part of a PC that stores programs and files that can be written to and read. Data remains secure when switched off, although *backups* are ALWAYS advisable. Hard disks are measured in megabytes (Mb) or gigabytes (Gb).

HARDWARE
The physical elements of a computer system such as the CPU, disk drive, printer, keyboard or monitor.

HYPERLINK
A part of Web page – usually a piece of text or image – that when clicked on automatically transfers the user to a different point within the same page, a different page or an entirely different Web site.

ICON
A small labelled symbol on the desktop or within folders that represents a file, program or command. Icons are usually activated by double-clicking.

INTERNET
A massive network of computers all linked together making it possible to exchange information. Often abbreviated as "the Net".

INTERNET EXPLORER
The Web browser which is installed with Windows 98.

INTERNET SERVICE PROVIDER (ISP)
A company that sells the facility to connect to the Internet. Most ISPs also provide the software necessary to access the Net.

LAN
Acronym for Local Area Network – usually a small network of computers linked within an office for the purposes of file sharing or communication.

MAXIMIZE
Expanding a window so that it fills the entire screen. You can do this by double-clicking on the title bar – the long strip at the top containing the window's name – or by clicking the <u>MAXIMIZE BOX</u> (the middle box on the top right hand corner).

MEMORY
Slightly ambiguous term that usually refers to the Random Access Memory (RAM), which stores whatever you're working on at that moment. Computers like to have a much RAM as possible to work efficiently.

MEGABYTE

Approximately one million bytes.

MENU BAR

The strip directly beneath the title bar that lists your options. Pointing and clicking at an item on the menu bar activates a drop-down menu containing commands. Specific menu bar contents will differ between programs.

MINIMIZE

Shrinking a window to its smallest possible size, so that it "disappears" and is shown only as an item on the task bar. The <u>MINIMIZE</u> button appears as a square with a horizontal line near the top right of the title bar.

MODEM

A "modulator/demodulator" – a piece of hardware used to transfer data between two computers across a telephone line. Modems can be external devices but are now more commonly built into the computer.

MONITOR

The screen which is connected to your PC.

MOTHERBOARD

The main circuit board in a computer.

MULTI-TASKING

The capability of a computer (or program) to allow several different tasks to be performed simultaneously.

NETWORK

A group of interconnected computers.

NEWBIE

Slightly derogative term given by experienced users to those who are new to the Internet or computers generally.

ONLINE

A term to describe a computer or user currently connected to the Internet or any other network. The reverse is "Offline".

OPERATING SYSTEM
The software that controls how a computer performs its most basic tasks, such as storing files or running other programs. Windows 98 is an example of an operating system.

PATH
The route through the various layers of folders that a computer has to take to locate a specific file. The path C:\My Documents\Correspondence\Letter X indicates that the document "Letter X" is in a folder called "Correspondence", which in turn is in a folder called "My Documents" stored on drive "C:".

PCI
Acronym for "Peripheral Component Interface", a type of expansion slot in which audio and video cards can be added for improved functionality.

PLUG AND PLAY
A protocol that makes it easy to add and configure additional components and devices to a PC.

PLUG-IN
A tiny add-on program that adds functionality to a Web browser, allowing you to play, for example, animations, videos or sound files.

PROGRAM
Software that enables you to perform specific tasks, such as word processing, creating spreadsheets or playing games. Without a program a computer can't do anything remotely useful.

READ ONLY
A type of file that can be read from but not written to.

RECYCLE BIN
A folder that stores files that have been removed from the hard disk.

RESOLUTION
A measurement that describes the number of visible pixels, the tiny dots on the screen that form the words and images that you see. A greater number of pixels means a higher screen resolution which creates a sharper image.

SCREEN SAVER

A program designed to activate when a computer has been idle for a period of time. Screen saver animations are deliberately designed to move around thus preventing the Desktop image "burning" into the screen when idle.

SCROLL BAR

The horizontal and vertical lines that sometimes appear on the bottom and right hand sides of a window to indicate that there is more content than currently shown. The unseen part of the page can be accessed by clicking on arrows at the end of each bar, on the bar itself or dragging the cursor downwards.

SEARCH ENGINE

A Web site that can be used to locate other Web sites by performing keyword searches. The most commonly used are Yahoo!, Excite, Lycos and AltaVista. Each system uses slightly different search criteria, so it's always worth trying different engines.

SHAREWARE

Software, usually developed by an individual or small company that can be downloaded from the Internet and sampled free of charge for a trial period.

SHORTCUT ICON

A user-defined desktop icon that can be used to provide immediate access to a program or file buried within the folder structure. They can be identified on the desktop by a tiny arrow in the bottom left-hand corner of the icon.

SHORTCUT KEY

An underlined letter in one of the drop-down options from a menu bar that can be used as a shortcut to executing the command.

SHUTDOWN

The process in which Windows 98 maintains its settings before a PC can safely be switched off. Always avoid turning off your computer without clicking on the SHUTDOWN option in the Windows 98 START menu.

START BUTTON

The button marked START usually found at the bottom left-hand corner of the Windows 98 screen which launches the Start menu.

START MENU

List of options which appears when you click <u>START</u>. Choosing from this list allows you to run programs, alter settings, load files or shut down. It can also be launched with ALT+ESC or from the special WINDOWS key which can be found on some keyboards.

STREAMING

A technique for playing audio or video files as they are being downloaded. A browser plug-in decompresses the signal and plays it back immediately meaning that you don't have to wait for the entire file to be downloaded.

SUBFOLDER

A folder within a folder.

TASKBAR

The bar that runs along the bottom of the screen containing the Windows 98 START button and indicates, among other things, the current programs that are running and folders that are open.

VIRUS

A tiny malicious program deliberately designed to corrupt data. Most are distributed via the Internet so it's always a good idea to run software from the Interent through virus-checking software first.

WALLPAPER

The picture that appears on the desktop. The Control Panel allows you to choose from a variety of wallpaper files, or you can create your own designs.

WEB SPACE

The free space your ISP allocates on its server for your own Web pages.

WIZARD

A Windows 98 program that provides step-by-step instructions and options to help you complete a task.

WORLD WIDE WEB

A vast collection of Web sites on the Internet that can be navigated using a Web browser and hypertext links.

INDEX